Practical Program Evaluations

Practical Program Evaluations
Getting from Ideas to Outcomes

Gerald Andrews Emison
Mississippi State University

CQ PRESS

A Division of Congressional Quarterly Inc.
Washington, D.C.

CQ Press
1255 22nd Street, NW, Suite 400
Washington, DC 20037

Phone: 202-729-1900; toll-free, 1-866-4CQ-PRESS (1-866-427-7737)

Web: www.cqpress.com

Cover design: Jeffrey Everett/El Jefe Design

∞ The paper used in this publication exceeds the requirements of the American National Standard for Information Sciences—Permanence of Paper for Printed Library Materials, ANSI Z39.48-1992.

Printed and bound in the United States of America

10 09 08 07 06   1 2 3 4 5

Library of Congress Cataloging-in-Publication Data

Emison, Gerald A.
  Practical program evaluations: getting from ideas to outcomes / Gerald Andrews Emison.
     p. cm.
  Includes bibliographical references and index.
  ISBN-13: 978-0-87289-302-3 (alk. paper)
  ISBN-10: 0-87289-302-2
  1. Public administration—Evaluation.   2. Administrative agencies—Evaluation.   I. Title.

  JF1351.E55 2007
  352.4'39—dc22   2006023238

To Robert and Carol Emison
and Grace and Beau,
whose memories guide me still

CONTENTS

TABLES, FIGURES, AND BOXES

PREFACE

Program evaluation is an important way to advance the public interest. It opens windows to improving the performance of public organizations. Performance in the public sector has always been a major concern, and the past decade has seen an increasing emphasis on it. Whether termed *reinventing government, new public management,* or *results-based management,* this new emphasis on results reflects the fact that achievement requires reflection, and program evaluation is institutionalized reflection. It enables the intellectual underbrush to be cleared away and performance improvements to be identified. This identification, however, is not enough for improvements to be realized; implementation is also necessary. This book concerns the practices that heighten the likelihood that a program evaluation will lead to implemented recommendations and subsequent improvement.

As a career member of the federal senior executive service for more than twenty years, I saw that two components typically made up successful program improvements. The first was rigorous, unbiased, and thorough analysis. The second was a series of practices that enabled decision makers to translate the analysis into change. The first component is the focus of most program evaluation texts and courses, whereas the second usually is left to "education by osmosis" when an evaluator begins work in the "real world." The focus on the former at the expense of the latter is easy to understand. Learning the tools and methodology of program evaluation is not easy, so teaching competency in these skills is crucial. Seemingly, the latter is really just good common sense and can be more easily taught on the fly. But what seems so obvious is often not so for students first entering the workforce.

It is not necessary to leave a critical aspect of successful evaluation to happenstance. This book identifies those practices that savvy evaluators follow so that their evaluations get implemented. It adds another dimension to the preparation, reflection, and practice that compose the essentials of program evaluation—a handy way to offer concrete advice and reinforce the practical.

The foundations of this book are my own experiences in the public sector and in the classroom. I initially conducted program evaluations as an analyst for the U.S. Environmental Protection Agency (EPA). As a manager, and later, as the director of the program evaluation division, I saw the effective, the ineffective, and the neglected as this group dealt with highly controversial issues. During this period I had many conversations with colleagues about what composed a truly worthwhile evaluation. Almost every practitioner spelled out successful change as the measure of a combination of rigor and practical action.

My work on evaluations led to my crossing over from evaluator to director of a large EPA regulatory program. As the director of air quality planning and standards, I found myself a customer of program evaluations and policy analyses. In this role I was able to observe, during my interactions with political executives and senior career appointee colleagues, what worked and what did not. This experience validated my belief that a combination of rigor with the practical is essential. When I moved to a regional office to become its senior career executive, my observations were reconfirmed in yet another venue. A good program evaluation needs conceptual rigor *and* practical application in order to be implemented.

Shortly after I left the regional office, I found myself teaching policy analysis in a university setting. As a practitioner I often had wondered why the practical skills essential for successful evaluations were so randomly distributed among newly graduated evaluators. I soon realized it was because most academic training in program evaluation emphasized conceptual preparation without much stress on practical pathways to success. When I retired from the senior executive service and became a full-time academic, I could not find a satisfactory text that exposed my students to this complementary aspect. So I wrote this book.

For those teaching introductory program evaluation courses, this book supplements the many fine core texts available. It introduces the practices essential to effectiveness in applied settings. It supplements, rather than replaces, the conceptual emphasis that is the staple of traditional program evaluation courses. The intention is to round out graduate students' education and preparation. Its most useful place is early in a graduate program evaluation course, when students can employ this guidance on the content of the course throughout a semester. The book also can serve as an accessible reference to remind practicing evaluators in the rush of day-to-day work what is important for effectiveness.

The book is organized to promote accessibility. Chapter 1 explains the reasoning behind the text and its relevance to today's program evaluator. Chapter 2 places the book in the terrain of the overall enterprise of program evaluation. The text's core lies in the next four chapters. Each examines a key attribute of successful practical program evaluations. The 4Cs—client, content, control, and communication—are used to bundle the essential practices and to examine a series of related practices in a framework that students can return to easily.

Since this book is practice based, it is impossible to thank adequately everyone who played a part; it is my exposure to many dedicated public officials that enabled me to write it. Nevertheless, there are a number of people who contributed mightily to my ideas. Ron Brand, first as my boss, then as my mentor and friend, contributed extensively to most of the ideas found within. Stan Meiburg, as a staff assistant and then a colleague, has never failed to shed new insight upon public evaluation. John Thillmann, David Ziegele, and Tom Kelly were always able to bring me back to earth and remind me that in the long run if a practice does not improve program performance, it is not worthy of extensive effort. And the staffs of the EPA's Office of Air Quality Planning and Standards in Washington, D.C.; Research Triangle Park, North Carolina; and the Seattle, Washington, regional office consistently demonstrated that long-run improvement of the public's interest was why we were in the game.

My colleagues at Mississippi State University deserve special thanks, since they provided both the models and the encouragement to pursue this project. Similarly, colleagues at Duke University gave me the opportunity to structure these ideas into a coherent package for the first time.

This work had its start in a conversation with Michael Dunaway of CQ Press. I am indebted to him for recognizing that there might be a book somewhere in my ramblings. Charisse Kiino has served as my guide and encourager at CQ Press, and this book simply would not exist without her counsel and encouragement. I am quite grateful for her persistence and patience. The production of the book was aided immeasurably by the thoughtful review of Abigail Harrison Emison. I also would like to thank the reviewers, whose supportive yet unvarnished critiques led to improvements that would not have occurred without their input: Daniel Baracskay, Valdosta State University; Steve Daniels, California State University at Bakersfield; Heidi Koenig, Northern Illinois University; Laura Langbein, American University; Tom Liou, University of Central Florida; Peter Mameli, City University of New York–John Jay College of Criminal Justice; Elizabethann O'Sullivan, North Carolina State University; and Dan Williams, City University of New York–Baruch College.

Last, I must thank the one person who has been a model of good humor and support, not only in the writing of this book but also in the experiences upon which this book draws. My wife, Donna Kay Harrison, has been for more than thirty years the litmus test for ideas on the practicality, humanity, and wisdom of major choices I have made in my career. Without her, not only would this book be impossible, the career that underlies it would have been impossible as well. I owe her a debt that is simply unpayable. But it is balanced, I hope, by a bottomless well of gratitude.

Such a wide range of contributors has allowed me to bring a number of experiences to this book. Nevertheless, while many helped, the work is mine alone, and I take responsibility for it while gratefully thanking everyone who helped directly or indirectly.

Practical Program Evaluations

PROGRAM EVALUATIONS THAT MATTER

Program evaluation concerns the core of public management: how public organizations can be effective in achieving society's interests while advancing democratic governance. It is simultaneously important, challenging, interesting, and exciting.

Program evaluation is important. It concerns the means by which society provides itself services unavailable through market mechanisms. It deals with topics as diverse as public assistance, environmental protection, public safety, national defense, education, and disease prevention. Effectively carrying out these and the other activities of public enterprise is vital because the impacts are widespread in society. Put simply, the decisions that are the focus of program evaluation have the potential to substantially improve people's lives if done well or harm these same lives if done poorly. This book aims to help you develop the skills that increase the chances of improving people's lives by strengthening public and non-profit organization performance effectively and responsibly.

Program evaluation is challenging. It calls for rational thought and adept synthesis of circumstance, theory, and method as well as communication that is effective. This is hard work when done well. We program evaluators must exercise our critical faculties in an interdisciplinary manner, use both our formal and informal knowledge, and then communicate the synthesis in a persuasive manner.

Program evaluation is interesting. It requires both clear thinking and creativity in managing public endeavors. Few textbook solutions are found in this work. To be sure, we must observe certain methodological verities. Success requires us to apply basic principles, and these principles must be thoughtfully brought to the unique circumstances of a program setting. But such circumstances almost always will combine a range of features, such as interpersonal, economic, political, organizational, legal, and scientific aspects of public programs. As a result, both well-grounded, thoughtful appraisal of the situation and flexibility in adapting basic principles and techniques to this situation demand that we bring a creative mind to the task.

Program evaluation is exciting. It concerns an ever-evolving effort to improve the functioning of endeavors to advance society's common interests. There are few activities in which we are required to stretch our analytic capabilities across such a broad terrain, be extraordinarily creative, speak and write persuasively, and to do this all in the service of helping society.

This book aims to provide practices that allow you to build on sound methodology through practical approaches that result in the use of program evaluations that advance the public interest.

THE MYTH OF CETERIS PARIBUS

The following cases have been changed slightly to keep them anonymous or highlight key features, but they are based on fact. Both concern program evaluations in public service. Both were conducted by highly motivated and intelligent evaluation team members for clients interested in their work.

Kate Payne tapped on Tom Edward's door. "I know it's almost six, but you got a minute? I just heard from Al Janes. The outpatient office wants to hold off on doing anything with my report. I'm so mad I can't see straight. That evaluation was well done, and they're just sitting on it."

Tom, the director of the program evaluation division, motioned Kate to a chair. "Well, Kate, I haven't been keeping up on this evaluation since Chris was the management team member looking after it. Fill me in a little, will you?"

"Well, you probably remember that the office wanted an evaluation of the performance of dialysis clinics so it could develop proposals for Congress to

consider." Tom nodded. "Well, we did a national data survey of over 200 clinics, stratified according to size and type of clients as well as type of dialysis. We then did a factor analysis of important influences and presented our findings to Al this afternoon. The results weren't as clear as he wanted. I think we may have been too prissy in our characterizations, but we still had some good ideas. Al was in a hurry and didn't give us a chance to explain the nuances. He just heard that there were complications and his eyes glazed over. Then he asked us to think about expanding the analysis and said that he'd have to wait and think about doing anything."

Kate continued, "This was a sound piece of work. But the client has stiffed us. Man, I'm fried. Why are we in this business? I'm sick of pushing a rope. I got into this to help people's health, and it seems all I'm doing is creating studies that go nowhere."

Marian's home phone rang at 7:30 p.m. It was Kelly Brown. He had just finished briefing the State of Fremont's assistant secretary of ecology for field operations on the study of Superfund resources and results. He was calling Marian from his car because he couldn't wait until the next day to tell her about the meeting. "Marian, she bought the whole thing. I laid out the results just like we'd talked about doing. Mary Anne said it was the most interesting information she'd had in the year since she'd become the assistant secretary. You were right. I was wrong. Nobody asked about a causal analysis or the validity of our data. Mary Anne just jumped in and began asking questions about why there was such disparity among the regions. I told her that we didn't know, that all we could do in the time she'd given us was use existing data and display the full-time equivalents and the construction completes. She didn't care. She was so happy to have a few facts that showed how the regions were doing that she immediately committed to launch the tiger team we recommended to catalogue the successful practices of the high-performing regions. You know, this was a small study, and I doubted that anything would come of it since it lacked the high-octane analysis we usually shoot for. But I guess you're right. In the land of the blind, the one-eyed man is really king."

Despite their similarities, these two cases were very different in their conduct and in their outcomes. One was executed using state-of-the-art analytic techniques yet was abandoned by the customer. The other, a success, was conducted using techniques that were old hat during the Harding administration. By contemporary program evaluation logic, the outcomes were counterintuitive. Shouldn't analytic precision trump ambiguity? Shouldn't crude analysis be a thing of the past and thrown out? Maybe and maybe not. Economists are fond of employing the maxim ceteris paribus, other things being equal. Perhaps, ceteris paribus, analytic horsepower and detailed data collection trump crude characterization; however, ceteris is rarely paribus. That is, things are rarely equal. Methodological rigor matters in program evaluation. But so do many other things.

PRACTICING PROGRAM EVALUATION IN A COMPLEX WORLD

Things other than methodological rigor are important because we evaluate programs in a complex world. We undertake program evaluations to enhance the performance of public efforts and thereby advance the public interest. While this is a straightforward intention, putting it into practice is anything but straightforward. This is because program evaluation reflects the complex characteristics of any social enterprise.

Program evaluation can be carried out in several places within an organization. If you can think of an organizational level that interacts with public activities, you can find a fruitful use for program evaluation. Multiple sectors may be involved. While program evaluation may concern itself with governmental performance, it is equally legitimate for nongovernmental organizations to be concerned with and to carry out evaluations. Private firms that contract with governments to deliver public programs undertake evaluations, as do private firms that may be regulated by public programs. Program evaluations are conducted at multiple levels of government. State, local, and federal governments fret about their programs' performance, and program evaluation can provide valuable insights into these concerns. Similarly, all three branches of government—executive, legislative, and judicial—are interested in program performance. So, institutional complexity typically characterizes evaluations.

Program evaluations also have multiple purposes, which adds to the complexity. At the conceptual level, performance enhancement is the purpose, but it covers many more specific intentions. Program evaluations can be undertaken to identify opportunities for management improvement. Managers seek better performance, and program evaluation techniques can yield insight into how that can be achieved. Evaluations can be used as a weapon to find fault with how a program is being conducted and thereby gain political advantage. Few public programs are flawless, and program evaluations can uncover problems and yield ample grounds for criticism, again, for political advantage. Or evaluations may be used to demonstrate that the initiating agent is committed to thoughtful analysis, even when there's little interest in altering a program. Doing the study instead of using the study can be the objective in such cases. What is likely, however, is that purposes may overlap, with both improvement and political advantage, for example, being sought. What is certain is that many valid purposes exist for program evaluations, and conducting them responsibly requires that program evaluators recognize the complexity this produces.

If the complexity deriving from multiple institutional venues and multiple purposes wasn't enough, evaluators also find themselves playing various roles as they execute the evaluations. The standard role is the evaluator as neutral analyst, concerned with the technically sound conduct of the evaluation. The analyst thus is a professional applying his or her skills in a manner that is independent of the evaluation's outcome. Another role is that of advocate, using methodologically unique skills to identify either positive or negative features of a public program to either advance or undermine the program, depending upon the nature of the evaluator's advocacy. In actuality, practicing evaluators often partially inhabit those two roles simultaneously. Sound conduct is often paired with a judgment that the evaluator reaches about the program as the evaluation rolls out. In such cases, neutral analysis must precede advocacy so that reliability leads preferences.

Such complexity of organizational venue, purpose, and roles interacts so that success in program evaluation often depends upon pragmatic practices. These practices frequently influence whether a program evaluation gets used regardless of venue, purpose, or role as well as the methodological purity of the work. Practicing program evaluators know a dirty little secret: Many things beyond scientific quality matter in whether an evaluation's recommendations get implemented. This does not mean that scientific quality does not matter. It does. A lot. Without scientific soundness, inquiries may or may not be valid; we can't tell for sure. And not being able to assess validity hamstrings program evaluation. But such complexity means we need to add something else to our conduct of program evaluations for them to be used. That is what this book is about: the something else.

WHY SHOULD YOU READ THIS BOOK?

If you examine the academic training for program evaluation in most contemporary graduate programs in public affairs, you will discover that, regardless of the text, the syllabus, and the field, the training emphasizes professional practices of sound data collection, rigorous analytic procedures, and careful explication of findings. These are important, but because of the complexity of real program evaluations, they are not enough. Program evaluations involve making choices, and the people who conduct the evaluations don't check their human natures at the door. As a result, many things get tossed into the decision-making process. That is as it should be because the complexity of program evaluation means that much more than methodology is essential to success. Rationality in decision making is but one of a variety of important considerations that matter in making choices. Yet program evaluation training in the public sector seems to have overlooked this inconvenient fact.

So what we often find in formal training in program evaluation is attention to rationality, rigor, and careful methods. All are foundationally important. Laying this foundation and getting graduate students the technical and methodological proficiency they need takes much time and energy, so the other dimension—the practical, human, messy aspect of decision making in program evaluation—does not get as much attention. Work starts and an analyst is faced with the realities of conducting and selling the results of a program evaluation. The experience of trial and error, or if the analyst is lucky, the tutelage of an old hand, helps influence whether a program evaluation gets used.

It can be frustrating when we spend so much effort, intellectual capacity, and caring only to see our evaluations disappear when we don't act based on the fact that complex humans produce and consume program evaluations. The situation is similar to spending time and thought developing menus and buying healthy foods to control your weight but then forgetting that unless the food can be prepared quickly and easily you are unlikely to eat it when you are hungry. Instead, you turn to the tortilla chips that are readily available.

THE PARADOX OF APPLIED PROGRAM EVALUATION

When I directed the program evaluation group at the Environmental Protection Agency, my colleagues and I were able to recruit some extraordinarily bright, educated, and motivated staffers. Invariably, however, they understood only part of the success equation for program evaluations. Their education had equipped them with the statistical tools and research methods to conduct first-rate program evaluations. Yet they were often clueless about the practical considerations that were essential to be effective. Being practical managers, we didn't ponder why the newcomers were not what they could be. We set about teaching these talented people what they needed to know and just moved on from there.

When I left government service to teach program evaluation in a university setting, I began to realize that our young tigers did not know these important things because they typically had not been told. I have written this book about the practices that a few instructors teach but that are rarely reinforced by traditional textbook material. Maybe the practices are so mundane that they are obvious. Maybe the practices are so atheoretic that they are not worthy of scholarship. Maybe the texts are written by those with experience mostly on the theoretical side. In any event, it doesn't matter. If the practices were so obvious, people wouldn't need to be instructed in them when they reach the real world. Even if not worthy of scholarship, they undercut those topics considered more worthy of scholarship and thus become crucial. While the textbooks written by scholars have mastered the theories, I believe they can be augmented so the theories lead more often to improved outcomes.

This book concerns those practices that are modest in concept but challenging in execution, will, perseverance, and implementation and are necessary to yield improvement. There are ways to cut through the complexity. It is like trying to lose ten pounds. Everyone who wants to lose ten pounds knows what needs to be done: Reduce calorie intake and increase exercise. It's simple, actually. Yet it is so hard. Program evaluation is conceptual rigor delivered through effective practices. To neglect either conceptual rigor or effective practices is to place our efforts at risk. We need both in program evaluations. Many fine textbooks exist concerning conceptual rigor. This book concerns effective practices.

THE CORE PRINCIPLES OF THE C⁴ APPROACH

We conduct program evaluations for many reasons. We may launch a program evaluation to improve the results of a program, lower the program's cost, identify opportunities for efficiencies, or demonstrate a commitment or opposition to the program. Across all these, the assumed purpose is improving performance. To improve performance, things must change. A popular definition of insanity is doing the same thing over and over yet expecting a different result. Program evaluations seek to impact what William James called the cash value of an activity, and they do so based on observable evidence, the essence of empiricism.[1]

Program evaluation is embedded in managing improvement. Peter Drucker says that effective executives are concerned principally with enhancing organizational performance.[2] Program evaluation provides a disciplined means for improving performance of public programs and, consequently, sits squarely in the management domain. As a result, anything that increases the likelihood of improvements is worthy of focus. More reliable data collection and more insightful analytic techniques merit attention because they improve the validity of the knowledge upon which improvement is based. Similarly, if specific practices enhance the likelihood that ideas for improvements can be translated into changes, they, too, are worthy of consideration.

Program evaluation practices that translate concepts into actions involve what I call the C⁴ Approach, with the four C's standing for client, content, control, and communication. Successfully attending to each is vital to get program evaluations not only conducted but also adopted. If we leave one out, we court irrelevance.

The first group of practices concerns the client. The client provides the purpose for the conduct of the evaluation. When we conduct program evaluations, it is almost always for our client. The key to success is understanding our client. This may be more difficult than it initially seems. Often we can be confronted with multiple clients, who may not have identical interests. For example, do we attend to the interests of the staff person who is the contact point within the organization or those of the senior executive for whom the staff person is acting? The staff person may be motivated by the need to complete the work in a timely fashion and stay within budget, while the executive's interests may be more substantive and involve measuring effectiveness and the sources of effectiveness for the program we're evaluating. Sorting this out requires that we think carefully about the underlying purpose of the evaluation. And if we don't do this well and keep it before us while we're navigating the program evaluation, we risk succeeding at the wrong task. Understanding the client's interests is essential to having a program evaluation that goes beyond study to action. The goal is implementation. Those who are in a position to see that a client organization implements change will bring it about only if they believe it is in their interest to do so. Don't think for a moment that you're doing this work for the purity of analysis. It has a purpose, and the client can provide that purpose.

The content of the analysis governs the substantive nature of the evaluation. We must attend to the actual material of the evaluation. This means we must understand how the important features of the program work. There is no substitute for knowing what you're doing. As a result, having command over the facts of the program and the methodological characteristics of the analysis are both essential.

If you are evaluating the adoption program for a human services agency, you must become an expert on the process of adoption. This means understanding the way the process works in practice, not in theory. If you are evaluating an air traffic control system, it will be necessary for you to know what the real work of the air traffic controllers is. This knowledge must be at the specific, practical, and tangible level. There is no substitute for knowing how things work, as opposed to how they are supposed to work.

Similarly, our command over analytic techniques must be masterful. Most program evaluation textbooks provide considerable information on this, and Chapter 2 provides an overview of these concepts. Suffice it to say that knowing what you are doing must start with knowing how to use analytic tools appropriately.

It will be impossible to gain agreement to undertake changes if we don't ground our recommendations in a solid understanding of the facts and processes of the program. And our analysis must be similarly grounded in competent methods. I cannot think of a worthy replacement for knowing what you are talking about, and focusing on the content of the analysis will assure that you do so.

The third C is control. Simply put, successful program evaluations are managed well. They are timely, stay within resources, do not generate unnecessary interpersonal differences, and draw from all assets the insights necessary to identify worthwhile improvements. Most program evaluations are complicated projects. They concern programs that can be multilayered, with overlapping interests and capabilities; they also can involve considerable ambiguity. Add to this evaluators who are often highly educated and opinionated, and the result is the prescription for a challenging project management. Savvy program evaluators recognize that the opportunities are considerable to get offtrack and run the evaluation across the ditch and into the field. Attention to the management structure of roles and responsibilities, the decision-making and conflict resolution processes, and the ongoing behaviors of team members is essential for success. There is no hope to have something implemented if it cannot be produced. Controlling the analysis from the outset can assure that a product will emerge for the client to consider.

Having a good idea is not enough. If that idea is not communicated understandably to someone who has the authority to do something about it, it might just as well not exist at all. The final C in program evaluation success is communication. Successful program evaluations, those that lead to adoption and change, are well communicated. Most clients are individuals who have too little time and too many demands to spend considerable effort figuring out what an evaluation says and means. We must communicate the evaluation in a manner that makes it easy for the client to understand the content, agree with the conclusions, and direct that actions be taken. None of this happens if the information is not well communicated. Furthermore, it does no good to operate on the basis of telling clients what they should do. Clients will do what they will do. Our job is to make it easy for them to do what we believe is appropriate, which means we must adequately communicate the program evaluation's results in a manner that persuades them to act.

AN X-RAY OF THE BOOK

Chapter 2 discusses the context for conducting program evaluation. It also identifies resources you can turn to for strengthening your theoretical foundations. The subsequent chapters are built around the four C's of the C⁴ Approach: client, content, control, and communication. A chapter is dedicated to each C and includes a focus on practices. For each practice, you will examine the core principle that motivates it. Then the discussion turns to why the particular principle matters, and a case is presented that illustrates the importance of the principle. These cases are based upon actual experiences. However, they should be viewed as hypothetical for illustrative purposes. To protect confidentiality or to highlight particular aspects of the cases, certain things have been changed. You explore the practical aspects of what action you can take to be true to the principle, things you should watch for that can trip you up, and what you can do when everything you have tried doesn't work.

By doing this for each of the practices that support the four C's, you build a portfolio of behaviors that can improve your chances of producing a program evaluation that leads to change and improvement.

OUR PURPOSE IS PROGRAM EVALUATIONS THAT MATTER

This is a modest book. It is not conceptually difficult, and most evaluators are capable of doing what it suggests. But many do not. Just because things are simple, that does not make them easy. Such is the case with program evaluations that matter. I have found that doing some basic things can lead to success. This book seeks to share the practices that can transform program evaluation into actual program improvement.

Whether as a conductor or later in my career as a client of program evaluations, I have consistently been amazed at how following some mundane practices dramatically improved implementation success, while neglecting to do these basic things had important adverse consequences. What follows shares these basic concepts.

While modest, this book is also outrageous. It proposes that when confronting complex situations, simple things matter and that sophisticated methodology is not enough. I believe that is true. For too long the program evaluation community has sent fledgling evaluators out to confront complex venues, purposes, and roles armed with scientific methodologies that are vital but, alone, are not enough. The consequence is a disconnect between conduct and contribution. I hope that this book helps direct the field more closely to contribution as the measure of success. When we bring knowledge and experience to bear on society's public problems through program evaluations, it is done so with the expectation of change and improvement under complex conditions. I believe that applying the C^4 Approach can both change and improve future program evaluations.

2

THE LANDSCAPE OF PROGRAM EVALUATION

Program evaluation uses rational processes to examine the conduct of a program in the public interest. We do this to assess the characteristics of a program and to improve its effectiveness.

This assessment and improvement are rooted in the history of using social science research to identify improvements in public programs.[1] As government programs proliferated in the New Deal of the 1930s, interest in determining the effectiveness of the programs increased, for both practical and political purposes. Empirical examination of the consequences of public activities emerged as a tool for understanding the relationships among purpose, methods, and outcomes for social programs. During World War II the use of empirical assessment for defense programs' effectiveness was accorded an even higher priority than that for social programs. When the war ended, the adaptation of assessment techniques to civilian purposes accelerated. During the 1940s and 1950s, the need for assessing government programs was heightened and thus more techniques were developed. With the application of the Planning, Programming, and Budgeting System (PPBS) of the 1960s, the formal assessment of program effectiveness was established. Despite the decline of PPBS, the use of empirical social science to examine and improve public activities became routine.[2] The expansion of social programs in the Great Society of the 1960s and the subsequent retrenchment employed program evaluation as a key means for assessing public program effectiveness. Today program evaluation is well established as a means for examining public program performance. However, the execution of this analysis has frequently faltered because of data unavailability, clients' unwillingness to probe the analysis, and impracticality of analytic techniques. Yet throughout the period of ascendancy of program evaluation, the unchanging core has been empirical examination of program effectiveness.

Examination depends upon evidence that logically supports the findings, and it never occurs in a vacuum. The context is always important to the design and conduct of evaluation work, and the C^4 Approach is intended to help you systematically engage the contexts necessary for a successful program evaluation, which frequently do not receive adequate attention. Before exploring each of the four C's, we need to see where this book fits on the intellectual terrain of public affairs broadly and program evaluation specifically. We can't reliably and flexibly use an approach unless we understand the context into which it fits.

THE PUBLIC INTEREST

The most prominent feature on the program evaluation landscape is the public interest. In the intellectual geology of program evaluation, it is the tectonic plate upon which all other features rest. Program evaluation seeks to advance the public interest, but what exactly is the public interest? We may think of the public interest as having two components. First, there is the instrumental achievement of a particular set of objectives that represent widely shared interests. Second, there is the adherence to a set of procedures that, if followed in selecting and pursuing objectives by society, yields an acceptable outcome for the group. Program evaluation seeks to advance achievement of public objectives while observing appropriate procedures within a democratic society.

What Is the Public Interest?

Think of the first component of the public interest as a substantive interest. What are those objectives worthy of pursuit by public means? Deborah Stone identifies a number of ways objectives can be developed in the public interest.[3] Interests that most members of a community want for themselves as individuals might be considered as in the public interest. For example, each person wants good health and to be free from environmental hazards. Another way the public interest may be expressed is pursuit of objectives that most members of a community hold for the community itself. The desire for sound public education typically is in the public interest for local governments. We may also think of the public interest as much more expansive, being composed of goals around which a community consensus can be formed. In essence, this is the viewpoint that whatever a community decides is in its interest is fair game for pursuit. This community-based approach can produce widely varying ideas of what constitutes the public interest. For example, some local governments have decided it is in the public interest for public schools to offer alternative views to the study of Darwinian evolution; other local governments have decided it is in their community's public interest to prohibit teaching all but Darwinian education.[4]

These definitions of the public interest are substantively based. The choice of a particular objective becomes the operational definition of the public interest. But there is another view of the public interest. It concerns the procedures for selection and pursuit of the public interest. This procedurally-based definition focuses on methods, not substance. Adherence to due process, established voting rules, transparency of information, and fair decision-making processes in themselves may be viewed as in the public interest, independent of the objectives selected as a result of these processes.[5]

Who Defines the Public Interest?

What actors define the public interest? Is it the polity, elected officials, trained professionals, particular interest groups, or some other group? For a program evaluator, this key question often can be answered only partially. In a democratic society the ultimate power for defining the public interest rests in the hands of the polity. But the polity rarely specifically addresses most programs and activities that are targets of program evaluations. The polity's broad expressions of public interest get cast into policy through the political process of selecting and holding accountable elected officials. Yet elected officials, too, may bring to the conversation their own broad statements of program objectives. They may then look to professionals familiar with particular programs and have them act as agents to transform broad program intentions and processes into specific actions that deliver the goods and services associated with the achievement of the public interest. And interest groups may provide the oversight that can keep programs on track. So, ultimately for those engaged in program evaluation, the question of who decides the public interest is an open-ended one. It depends on the situation and the context. In essence evaluators must constantly be conducting a conversation in their heads, asking what really is in the public interest and who most legitimately expresses that interest.

Measuring the Public Interest

Evaluators often confront the question of how to measure the accomplishment of a public interest objective. In many ways this measurement depends on how the public interest has been defined. If, on the one hand, it is defined as achieving certain individual goals, then aggregating those individual levels across the community can yield the measurement relevant to the public interest. If, on the other hand, it concerns goals for the community itself, then the standard for measurement must start at the aggregate community, not the individual, level. In such cases, expressions of the public interest are derived from particular instrumental social objectives.[6] In most cases there are two categories of measurement at play. The first concerns effectiveness of the program: How well does the program achieve the public interest? The second concerns efficiency: Are the costs of delivering the program acceptable in light of program objectives? The two objectives of effectiveness and efficiency typically compose the instrumental measurements for achieving the public interest in program evaluations.

If the public interest has been defined in terms of procedural acceptability, we can gauge the public interest from how well the procedures used to establish and pursue the objectives follow earlier agreed-upon processes. As a young analyst for a county council, I once asked the council staff director to describe an emergency upon which the council could act without the county executive's recommendation. "Whatever five members of the council decide is an emergency is an emergency" was his answer. The determination of the public interest was derived in this situation from a procedure established by a legitimate body.

Limits on the Public Interest

A number of critiques have been made of the concept of the public interest. Most stem from the assertion that it is not possible to aggregate group preferences in an impartial and reliable manner.[7] These critiques assert that the concept of public interest lacks a substantive empirical content and is a screen for promoting special interests. As a consequence, the concept allows the powerful to impose their values on those less advantageously situated.[8] These can be legitimate critiques, and program evaluators wisely recognize such limitations as influencing the public interest. The critiques are stronger, however, in their examination of deficiencies in the concept of public interest than in describing how aggregate social action in the larger interest could proceed. As a consequence, a thoughtful program evaluator is aware of the critiques in pursuit of evaluations that advance the public interest. And at the same time he or she recognizes that the public interest is revealed through imperfect action and that, despite criticisms, program evaluations improving the public's conditions can, if competently done, advance the public interest.

PURSUING THE PUBLIC INTEREST THROUGH RATIONALITY

Program evaluation's most prominent feature is rationality. Assessing the success of programs is the predominant means for program evaluation to advance the public interest. Program evaluation steadfastly acts on the basis that rationally connecting objectives, means, and outcomes can improve the outcomes and, consequently, the public interest. This is instrumental rationality. Other forms of rationality exist. Procedural rationality concerns following logical procedures, and communicative rationality concerns engaging in accurate, free, and unbiased communication.[9] Each type of rationality is important, but it is instrumental rationality that grounds program evaluation.

Instrumental Rationality's Heritage

Instrumental rationality is built upon the heritage of the rational decision-making model.[10] This model of decision making begins with identification of a problem requiring a choice to improve (see Figure 2-1). Based on this, the next step in the process specifies the goals, objectives, and criteria needed to achieve as a result of the choice. After describing what the general properties of a solution are, alternative paths are listed for solving the problem. Spelling out what an acceptable solution would look like (goals, objectives, and criteria) is done separately

FIGURE 2-1 **The Rational Decision-Making Model**

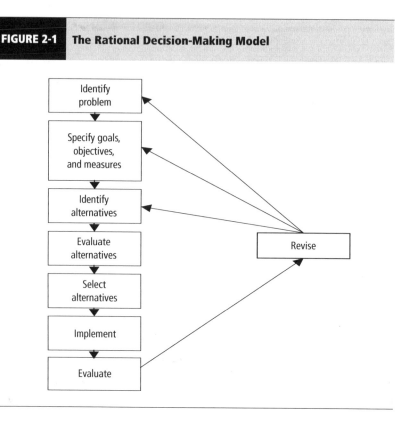

from actions that might meet those criteria (alternative generation). Next, the alternatives are evaluated using the measures of an acceptable solution and then compared. The preferred one is selected. With this selection, the model calls for implementation of the alternative accompanied by tracking to see how well it meets the goals, objectives, and criteria established at the outset. Based on this evaluation, further insight is used to inform revising the problem statement, the criteria, or the alternative. Thomas Dewey made this model the core of pragmatism, and it provides a logical means to relate purpose, methods, and learning.[11]

Instrumental Rationality's Limitations

When instrumental rationality works, it allows us to relate ends with means so that achieving the ends becomes more likely. But we must be aware of some niceties for this powerful process to work. We must be accurate, complete, and honest with ourselves in describing the nature of the problem and the goals derived from the problem statement. An old truism says: "If you don't know where you're going, any road will get you there." Even if we can describe our problem and the related goals, we must devise specific and tangible measures that can be used to gauge choices and outcomes. That means our objectives and criteria have to be as specific as possible and as measurable as possible. The identification of alternatives requires a familiarity with the potential solutions and a certain creativity so as not to overlook unconventional options. The techniques for assessing alternatives are similar to those of assessing the implementation of alternatives. In fact, program evaluation's intellectual home is in the phase of assessing the implementation of an alternative.

Assessing Instrumental Rationality

Assessment techniques can cover a wide range of activities. Descriptive characterization can provide insight into the worthiness of an alternative.[12] Program logic modeling can reveal the degree to which a program design rationally relates its parts to achieving a purpose.[13] Economic evaluation approaches such as cost-effectiveness and cost-benefit analysis can yield information about the efficiency of the alternatives' resources.[14]

A chief obstacle encountered in assessment concerns multiple objectives and multiple characterizations of achieving the objectives. To assess effectively we must be able to accurately identify the important consequences. This requires knowledge that may not be feasible to obtain. Further, in a public program's activities, we often face incommensurable measures of success. For example, we may want to improve children's educational performance and do so at low cost. How do you compare alternatives in which each has a different kind of measurement? One success measure can be testing scores and the other dollars expended. Choosing among alternatives requires mixing measurements. In short, public decisions, because they are public, almost always involve multiple objectives. How do we analyze and compare alternatives in the rational process? The answer is very carefully, because limitations exist as to how various techniques for analysis are employed.

Nevertheless, using rationality in many ways is similar to British prime minister Winston S. Churchill's characterization of democracy: "Democracy is the worst form of government, except all those other forms that have been tried from time to time."[15] Instrumental rationality in pursuit of the public interest is the most limited way to improve programs, excepting all others.

Categories of Instrumental Rationality

Instrumental rationality comes in two varieties: synoptic rationality and incremental rationality. Each can have considerable impact on approaching program evaluation, and each employs rationality. But how rationality is employed is different in each case.

Synoptic rationality requires that the knowledge necessary for successful use of the rational model be exhaustive. The decision maker must know the most important objectives and criteria associated with particular problems and goals, as well as be fully aware of all the relevant and available alternatives. In addition, synoptic rationality expects the consequences of each alternative to be completely described in the course of the evaluation processes.

Such comprehensiveness ignores the considerable price paid for acquiring such information.[16] From a practical standpoint, decision makers may make a good-faith effort to gather all this information, but the cost of being certain that any possible relevant information has been acquired is unrealistic given limits on time and resources that can be devoted to the task. This critique of synoptic rationality led Herbert Simon, Robert A. Dahl, David Braybrooke and Charles E. Lindblom, and others to advance the incremental view of rational decision making.[17] These incrementalists assert that when people make decisions they do not behave according to the requirements of synoptic rationality, simply because it is unrealistic to do so. Instead, according to this view, people make incremental decisions with the best information reasonably available, learn from the outcome, and then adjust accordingly.[18] Successive limited approximations of choices that lead toward the objective are a more accurate characterization of actual decision making.[19]

Whether operating from a synoptic or an incremental viewpoint, program evaluation depends upon rationality as its intellectual base. The ability to logically relate actions with outcomes is ⸻ promise.

DELVING INTO PROGRAM EVALUATION

Once we look more closely at the concept of rationalit ⸻ for feature on the landscape of program evaluation, other program evaluation elements become more distinct. Earlier we defined program evaluation as the use of rational processes to examine the conduct of a program in the public interest and assess its characteristics and effectiveness along with the sources of these qualities. Looking more closely, the real work associated with rational evaluations may be thought of as being carried out in three general areas: designing the evaluation, collecting data, and analyzing the data.

These combine to yield an interlocking set of activities that compose program evaluation. A number of valuable references examine in more detail the relationships of the components of program evaluation. A comprehensive discussion of the overall structure is available in a book by Peter H. Rossi, Howard E. Freeman, and Mark W. Lipsey, which stresses the relationship between concepts and processes in program evaluation.[20] For those seeking an integrated view of design and methods, the work of Richard D. Bingham and Claire L. Felbinger should be examined.[21] A less methodologically driven, yet comprehensive, treatment of the overall evaluation process is available in the book by Jody L. Fitzpatrick, James R. Sanders, and Blaine R. Worthen.[22] All these works provide accessible and detailed treatments of the program research activity and are excellent resources for those wishing more in-depth treatment of the overall subject. Each stresses the importance of combining intellectual rigor with a broad view of program evaluation's activities. For a consideration of how program evaluation activities fit together, Richard Berk and Peter H. Rossi's work may be profitably considered.[23] Earl Babbie and Martin Bulmer provide a more social science research perspective that can be related to evaluation design for those seeking a more theoretical viewpoint.[24]

Designing the Program Evaluation

Designing the evaluation develops the logic and the activities necessary to examine the program.[25] It is the skeleton of the evaluation, and every-ing else hangs on it. Think of it as deciding how to go about uncovering the important characteristics of a program and how to make the comparisons that can yield the insights we need for conducting an evaluation. There are multiple ways to do this. Fitzpatrick, Sanders, and Worthen identified at least five approaches to use, depending upon the purpose and the subject of the evaluation.[26] These concern either singly or in combination a program's objectives, its management, the consumers of the program, the expertise employed, and the participants. The choice of design would be strongly influenced by the particular approach chosen. John A. McLaughlin and Gretchen B. Jordan recommend employing program logic models to gain insight into the research design task.[27] These models seek to identify the logical flow of decisions and behaviors upon which programs are based. It is essential to understand the program's theory to choose how to evaluate it. Whether the evaluator uses a simple declarative statement of program assumptions or a more formal logic model, all program evaluation research designs begin with an implicit or explicit picture of the nature of the program and its relation to the evaluation task. In essence, use of program logic models is the specific subset of what Rossi, Freeman, and Lipsey term "program theory."[28] This is the effort to initiate evaluation from a conceptual basis to identify more generalizable insights that might be uncovered in the course of the evaluation. The more explicit are the assumptions about a program, the more accurate is the understanding of the program's theory.

The heart of evaluation design concerns spelling out the particular questions to be explored and the methods used for such exploration. One set of questions involves describing in detail a program's properties. For such efforts, fundamental statistical analysis, such as discussed by Hubert M. Blalock, William L. Hays, and authors of other social science statistics texts, can be invaluable for ensuring descriptive methods are valid.[29] Logic models describe a program's core processes and can help us focus on the key features necessary for a reliable design and implementation analysis. Rossi, Freeman, and Lipsey and Arnold Love discuss such approaches in detail.[30] This can focus on the relationship between identifying activities and their consequences.

A different category of questions around which an evaluation may be designed concerns causal relationships. This is the effort to relate interventions and outcomes, and quasi-experimentation plays a large role in such efforts. Selecting treatment and control groups and specifying the particular treatment studied to relate cause and effect are at the core of quasi-experimentation. The design of quasi-experiments is addressed in Donald Campbell and Julian Stanley's seminal work as well as Thomas Cook and Campbell's more extensive treatment of quasi-experimentation.[31] Charles S. Reichardt and Melvin M. Mark provide a highly accessible and concise discussion of quasi-experimentation for evaluation designers.[32]

Another dimension along which evaluations may be considered is whether and how they use quantitative or qualitative approaches. While quantitative analysis can yield more precise information, qualitative methods provide a richer, more nuanced picture of the conduct of a program. Blalock can provide an entry point for evaluation designers into quantitative analysis, and William H. Greene treats econometric examination of causal relationships comprehensively.[33] Sharon L. Caudle can provide a designer with an overview of the important considerations in deploying qualitative design.[34] Anselem Strauss and Juliet Corbin, Matthew B. Miles and A. Michael Huberman, and Joseph Maxwell provide more in-depth examination of key features of incorporating qualitative research into evaluation designs.[35] A particularly prevalent form of qualitative research in evaluations is the use of case studies. Exploring a particular situation can provide evaluators in-depth insight into program characteristics, processes, and consequences. An excellent, concise compilation of approaches for such case studies is Robert K. Yin's work.[36] At a more conceptual level Joe R. Feagin, Anthony M. Orum, and Gideon Sjoberg provide a multi-author exploration of the strengths and weaknesses of case studies in overall social science research.[37]

Programs are rarely tidy and evaluations of programs can mirror this fuzziness. As a result, designs typically concern mixed methods. They draw together qualitative and quantitative methods to yield descriptive evaluations and causal evaluations in various combinations. Fitzpatrick, Sanders, and Worthen explore the use of mixed methods especially from a qualitative-quantitative perspective, and Melvin M. Mark and R. Lance Shotland provide a more expansive treatment of combining methods to uncover insights about programs.[38]

Whether descriptive or causal in purpose, qualitative or quantitative in technique, or mixed in multiple dimensions, the design of the program

evaluation sets the course for the enterprise. Careful reflection at the outset on the methods as they relate to the purposes of the evaluation stands
you in good stead as you look more closely at evaluation activities.

Data Collection

The rational processes that are the foundation of program evaluation
depend upon accurate information. The data collection activity is critical
to have reliable information upon which to ground the evaluation. The
terrain of program evaluation data collection has twin peaks of data collection: qualitative data and quantitative data. Each peak is distinct from
the other, yet they are close enough to share a similar common foundation. That foundation is the need for accuracy, for data that validly depict
the phenomena under study.

The first peak of data collection is qualitative data. Think of qualitative
data as information derived from the interaction and ongoing adjust-
ment between the evaluator and the subjects under study. The works of
Caudle and Michael Patton are two sources that provide extensive dis-
cussions of the characteristics of qualitative data collection.[39] At the core
the evaluator collects information such that the topics explored are
adjusted as the data collection proceeds.[40] This requires close-up, careful
observation that seeks to identify relevant patterns.[41] For this to take
place the evaluator must focus on the natural world and observe occur-
rences first hand.[42] Context becomes important under such conditions.
Inquiry rests upon the condition that description can yield understanding.[43] As a consequence the foundation of qualitative data collection is
characterization of a program through subjective, descriptive means.

Evaluators must bring to such data collection a range of skills unique
to qualitative analysis. Fundamental is an ability to ask questions without
injecting bias into the responses. Further, evaluators who employ qualitative methods must be able to pose follow-up questions to subjects so that
information builds on previous responses.[44] These conditions require a
special preparation unique to qualitative conditions for successful data
collection. Pre-understanding of problems, processes, and contexts for
the program being evaluated are essential.[45]

Caudle has identified four general categories of qualitative data collection: direct observation, examining documents, interviews, and data

reduction into coherent patterns.[46] Wholey, Hatry, and Newcomer provide helpful advice on specific approaches for qualitative data collection.[47] From various perspectives, they discuss content analysis (the categorical coding of source documents), expert judgment (the organized assembly of experts' views), focus groups (client discussion around specific topics), and role playing (the observation of behavior in an artificial setting). Each of these approaches employs specific data collection techniques. Such techniques for content analysis are elaborated upon in works by Yvonna Lincoln and Egon Guba, Matthew B. Miles and A. Michael Huberman, and Earl Babbie.[48] George Geis, Harvey Averch, and Cynthia Weston discuss barriers and opportunities arising for using expert judgment in qualitative research.[49] Margery Austin Turner and Wendy Zimmerman provide a sound overview of role playing, and focus groups have been similarly treated by Debra L. Dean.[50] These sources can provide an introduction to particular techniques that compose part of qualitative data collection.

The second peak of data collection is quantitative data. Quantitative data are those observations that can be expressed through enumeration. It is important to ensure that the method for expression of enumeration matches the subsequently employed analytic technique.[51] For practical purposes, quantitative data are those that may be subjected to examination through the use of statistics. Consequently, data collection for quantitative analysis strives to attach enumeration to observations so various statistical analytic techniques may be deployed on the data. As a consequence a sound statistics textbook is extraordinarily helpful in designing quantitative data analysis. Blalock, Hays, and Greene have written three widely used references for this purpose.[52] However, hundreds of texts competently examine the use of statistics in research and analysis. Reference to these can vastly inform an evaluator's collection of quantitative data. Kathryn E. Newcomer and Philip W. Wirtz provide a concise summary of statistical uses that must be considered when preparing for quantitative data collection.[53]

Quantitative data may be collected directly from sources through the use of surveys, interviews, and otherwise direct observation in the field.[54] A broad examination of the issues in collecting evaluation data also may be found in Leigh Burstein, Howard Freeman, and Peter H. Rossi's work.[55] In general, emphasis on the accuracy of the sample in reflecting the population as well as the measurement of concept such that the underlying phenomenon is validly characterized compose the foundation of quantitative data collection.[56] These topics are examined in more detail by Floyd J. Fowler and Arlene Fink and Jacqueline Kosecoff (surveys) and by Seymour Sudman and Norman M. Bradburn (interviews).[57]

Secondary data collection concerns using data collected by sources other than the evaluator. In essence, it is piggy-backing on data collected for a purpose other than the one specified in the evaluation.[58] The obvious difficulty encountered with secondary data is the scope or definition of the measures reported upon may not match those of interest to the evaluator. The advantage is the ease and lower cost associated with such data collection.[59]

Analytic Approaches and Techniques

Many analytic approaches and techniques are available to the evaluator for examining data to identify relevant insights. The distinction between data collection and data analysis is blurry. Selecting data collection techniques requires and often foreordains the type of analysis undertaken. And if a particular analytic tool is to be employed, that may require specific types of data to be collected. As a consequence, the selection of data and the analytic techniques that will be applied to the data are codependent and must be in harmony.[60]

Analysis may be thought of as falling into two broad categories. First is analysis that characterizes the program and its relevant properties. Second is analysis that seeks to relate properties and consequences of the program. Regardless of type of analysis, the purpose is to obtain insight into the program with regard to effectiveness and efficiency.

Characterization of a program can involve diagrams, graphs, charts, and descriptive statistics. The underlying idea is that a careful and accurate characterization can reveal properties that are important to program performance but would otherwise be obscured without this descriptive analysis.

Edward R. Tufte provides a comprehensive explanation of using visual information to assist in understanding complex activities.[61] One of his works introduces best practices as well as fundamental principles of graphical depiction that assist analysis. Another provides a more conceptual treatment of the techniques that are most successful in visual analysis, and yet another integrates concepts and practices with advice for approaching specific analytic situations. A more irreverent and easily accessible treatment of the use of charts, graphs, and other visual information to convey (or mis-convey) concepts may be found in Gerald E. Jones's *How to Lie with Charts*.[62] He takes the inverted approach of showing how visual depictions can be manipulated to mislead the reader. In doing so he provides practical advice for ensuring that such things be accurate and clearly understood.

Descriptive statistics provide a more abstract means of characterizing programs. Most conventional statistics texts provide detailed treatment of the conventional measures of range, mean, median, mode, and so on that are the starting point for descriptive statistics. Correlations between factors in a program also may be useful in describing a program and can serve as a gateway to examining the causal relationships among important variables. These practices can be extended through the use of variations on regression analysis such as ordinary least squares, generalized least squares, logit, probit, and least squares dummy variable regression analysis. Texts such as those written by Blalock, Hays, and Greene can provide fundamental access to these statistical concepts.[63] An interesting companion to such conventional texts is Darrell Huff's *How to Lie with Statistics*.[64] As Jones does, Huff takes an irreverent approach so that the reader can learn to accurately employ challenging tools. For those looking for an easily accessible explanation of statistical concepts, John L. Phillips Jr. provides a concise treatment of basic statistical concepts.[65]

Examining the consequences, relationships, and effects of public programs can employ a range of quantitative techniques. Most conventional program evaluation textbooks provide a survey and introduction to these techniques. Wholey, Hatry, and Newcomer; Rossi, Freeman, and Lipsey; Fitzpatrick, Sanders, and Worthen; and McDavid and Hawthorn are some with especially comprehensive or accessible treatments of such quantitative techniques.[66] In particular Newcomer and Wirtz provide an overview of applying quantitative analysis to program evaluations.[67] James Edwin Kee's discussion as well as Henry M. Levin's explanation of benefit-cost analysis, Dale E. Berger's material on regression analysis, and Lawrence B. Mohr's review of impact analysis all provide more in-depth treatment of particular quantitative techniques.[68]

Recent use of program logic models and the Office of Management and Budget's Program Assessment Rating Tool are analytic tools that bridge qualitative and quantitative analysis to connect program actions with intended results.[69] These employ quantitative characterization combined with logical relationships between a program's efforts and outcomes to advance the routine assessment of program success in a management setting.

THE FOUR C'S AND THE LANDSCAPE OF PROGRAM EVALUATION

The landscape of program evaluation provides a setting for pursuing effectiveness through the C^4 Approach. Instrumental rationality is used by the evaluator to pursue the public interest through improving public programs. The activities of designing program evaluations, collecting data, and analyzing programs are the fundamental activities by which this pursuit of the public interest takes place. But the specifics of how this is carried out can make all the difference in the world between theoretically sound but ineffective evaluations and theoretically sound and effective evaluations.

UNDERSTAND YOUR CLIENT

For two reasons, your client is the key influence on whether a program evaluation's findings are adopted and implemented. First, and most obviously, the client is the one who sought the evaluation. If your findings are to improve the program's performance, it is likely the client who sees that the action occurs to make change happen. Second, even if your client is not the one who sees the work into the implementation phase, your orientation can affect the client's posture. And how the client feels can influence whether another party acts to implement your recommendations. In either case, if you attend to your client thoughtfully, carefully, and explicitly, you likely enhance the chances for transitioning successfully from studying to implementing the recommendations. To do this, you must have an accurate and sustaining understanding of your client.

Different clients play different roles. Legislators are different from political executives. And the roles are different from the role of program manager, program client, and program stakeholder. And, yes, the evaluator in some circumstances can become a client.

Clients can be motivated for all sorts of reasons to seek a program evaluation. Improving the operational conduct of a program can prompt an evaluation. Raising the efficiency or the effectiveness of a public activity is something that most clients would endorse even when it is not their primary objective. Similarly, the desire to influence overall program direction holds considerable interest for many actors as does laying the basis for long-range change. Clients can learn from the information provided

TABLE 3-1	Roles and Motivations of Clients in Program Evaluations

Motivation for seeking program evaluation

ACTOR	Improve operational program	Influence program direction	Gain knowledge of program	Justify prior decision	Lay basis for long-term change	Demon-strate scrutiny	Draw attention to program
Legislature	−	+	+	−	+	+	−
Political executive	−	+	−	+	−	+	+
Program manager	+	−	−	+	+	−	+
Program client	−	+	−	−	+	−	+
Stakeholder	−	+	−	−	+	+	+
Program evaluator	+	+	+	−	+	−	−

Note: + = More likely; − = Less likely.

during an evaluation, so gaining more knowledge of the program generally can be of interest. Sometimes demonstrating program control through scrutiny can be a way for an actor responsible for a program to fend off hostile intervention or remind people who is the boss. Actors with direct operational control often use evaluations as a means to justify a prior decision. And drawing attention to the program may cause some actors to seek an evaluation. While any client could be motivated by any of these purposes, different clients are moved to act more by some than others. Table 3-1 provides an overview of the relationships between various actors' roles and likely strength of different motivations.

KNOW WHAT YOUR CLIENT'S INTERESTS ARE

What matters most to the client is his or her interests. You must constantly be knowledgeable about your client's concerns and objectives. A

BOX 3-1	The Client Practices

Know What Your Client's Interests Are

Know What Success Is

Have a Principal Who Can Do Something

Put the Evaluation in a Management Context

Do the Right Thing

---

purpose always is behind the request for an evaluation. You must learn what that purpose is. And you must learn what the actual, not the stated, need is. Sometimes they are the same; sometimes they are different. Regardless, it is vital to know what the real purpose the client has for requesting the study. This means you must understand where your client's important interests lie.

These interests can take two primary forms: personal and programmatic. Personal interests are those derived primarily from the client's individual objectives. Programmatic interests are those that relate to the performance of the program under evaluation. Another way to think of these two types of interests is that personal interests are those particular to an individual while programmatic interests are those related to a larger public interest achieved through program performance. If you want to be effective, you need to understand each category of interest. Sometimes they will merge. A successful program can bring credit to its manager. Doing well by doing good is a characteristic of this scenario. Typically, the two types of interests are present to a greater or lesser degree and may overlap some, but not completely. This means you need to be explicit in your understanding of the client's interests and make honest distinctions of such interests. Having a professional interest in improving the public interest means a program evaluator may wish to accord less weight to personal interests. Nevertheless it is seriously unwise to ignore a client's personal interests. Identify both types of interests as you undertake the evaluation, keep a sharp lookout for how each is affected as you conduct the study, and, most important, continuously be aware of your client's personal and programmatic interests because doing so is important to the success of your evaluation.

Knowing your client's interests is essential because he or she will move to implement only recommendations that support those interests. Program evaluations should lead to improvement, and when that improvement requires client action, such action occurs only when it matches interests. You can save yourself considerable effort and heartache by knowing the client's interests. A realistic understanding of your client's interests reveals what could be profitably pushed and what is useless. While you still may advance recommendations that conflict with the client's interests, by being specifically aware of them, you are prepared for and not surprised by the conflict that can arise in such situations.

A client's interests may be complex, and figuring them out can be a headache. A client may have multiple, simultaneous interests that conflict. For example, a principal may wish to improve program performance but may take action only without changing budget requirements, operating principles, staffing, and organizational structures. In such cases your surest course of action is to identify all the interests, illuminate conflicts, and engage the client in confronting the contrary goals or interests. You may be able to do so at the outset. However, frequently such conflicts may not be apparent until the project unfolds. In those cases it is important for you to work through the conflicts with the client. Do not try to resolve the differences yourself. This situation is one that goes to the heart of the client's interests, and resolution of those conflicting interests belongs with the client.

Another layer of complexity in identifying and acting in harmony with a client's interest concerns multiple clients with dissimilar interests. Most public programs have more than one stakeholder, and each stakeholder can have a different interest. How do you handle such conflicts? First, try to identify if there is an overarching interest that all stakeholders share. Second, determine if one stakeholder's interests are so paramount that you should put those ahead of the others. In such cases your course of action may be clear when you prioritize the interests.

But what if the multiple clients have interests that conflict and each holds about the same priority? Take refuge in alternatives. Get the baseline data and then analyze the program using each client's predominant interest to shape one alternative. Use multiple measures of success that reflect all of the clients' interests. In this way you can guarantee that no legitimate interest gets overlooked, and you can focus the discussion of conflicts between clients upon concrete outcomes instead of more abstract values and interests. With multiple ways to look at the program you can bring light to each of the multiple viewpoints.

These differences are particularly sharp when public and private clients are juxtaposed. Public sector clients typically are focused on program consequences that are distributed across the community. Private sector clients are more concerned about particular impacts on unique parties. Examining both, should they hold equal status and valuation, can serve to highlight the real choices the principals face as a result of the evaluation.

The Case of the Open Space Program

Program evaluation is not just for governments; civic groups can use it to advance their interests. A keen understanding of client interests is essential regardless of the venue. The City of Collegeville in the southeastern United States in the 1990s established a program to purchase open space and trails land. Collegeville was growing and, like many American cities, development was gobbling up land. The city and county governments combined forces to create a citizens advisory panel, the Collegeville Open Space and Trails Commission, to supervise the selection of tracts to be purchased with government bonds. The group collaborated with related interest groups, particularly environmental ones, to advocate for protection of undeveloped sites and construction of walking and biking trails. At the same time, Collegeville was experiencing redevelopment of its central business district, and the city government, as in many cities, was encouraging private development in the district through construction of public facilities. These two interests collided, and an evaluation of the open space and trails program based on interests was key in settling the conflict between a citizens group and the city's redevelopment bureaucracy.

A developer of highly attractive residential conversions of industrial space in downtown Collegeville proposed to convert vacant warehouses into apartments but, to make them profitable, needed the city to reconstruct a substantial number of sidewalks and parking facilities. The city government proposed that the sidewalks and parking lots be built with funds from the open space and trails bond issue. The citizens group objected. The issue was resolved when a program evaluation of previous open space projects showed that no other project had ever been used to construct sidewalks and parking lots. The evaluation was done by citizen members of the commission who had a keen understanding of the specific interests of the group. By employing fact-based program evaluation of a descriptive nature, the citizens group was able to get the city government bureaucracy to drop the effort to divert bond funds away from purchasing open space and into developer support. The attention to interests was particularly important in this case. By showing the contrast between previous projects and the proposed assistance to the developer, the interests at play were publicly contrasted. This prompted the economic development hierarchy to drop its plans to raid the open space funds.

How to Proceed

The place to start discovering the client's interests is to ask. During the entrance interview with the client, you should at least ask questions along the lines of these: Why do you want us to do this work? What problems do you want this evaluation to fix? What do you envision coming out of this evaluation? It's six months from now, and we're sitting around congratulating ourselves on a program evaluation that succeeded beyond anyone's expectations. What does a successful program evaluation look like in this case? How was success attained?

It is important to listen carefully to the client when you pose these questions. Do not simply look for verification of what you believe to be his or her interests. Attend carefully to the client's description of both the problems to fix and the description of success.

Discovery of a client's interests is not a single-shot affair. The actual interests may take time to reveal themselves. Your client may be interested in something that is considered inappropriate. You need to find out what it is and do so without judging. For example, program evaluations can be sought as a justification to change a personnel assignment or reorganize a group. Clients usually are reluctant to express directly such interests. In that case, your personal style must be reassuring and relaxed to build rapport with the client that will bring out these interests.

The client is not the only window to interests and objectives. Program evaluations take place within organizations, and these organizations are populated with many people. Also, evaluations typically have stakeholders from outside the organization who are concerned about the program performance. It is important to seek the views of the important stakeholders about interests. This can involve a multistep process. First, you need to learn who the real players are. Power and influence are distributed formally and informally within an organization. Learning who holds the relevant power and influence in the organization for the program under evaluation is a vital task. It is especially important to attend to the informal influence based on specific, substantive program knowledge and personal relationships. They can provide keen insight that would not be suggested by looking at a simple organization chart. The same is true for those stakeholders who reside outside the formal framework of the organization. Public activities usually involve a diverse set of interests. Querying those interests can provide insight into the real interests at play in the evaluation.

What to Watch Out For

The big danger is getting too narrow a picture of interests. You must not settle simply for what the client says but examine what behaviors reveal to be the interests. You must not listen only to what stakeholders express but consider actions as windows to their real interests. In all cases you have to continually ask yourself: Do I have an accurate picture of the interests at play? Are there other actors with interests, and how do those interests interact with the client's? It is likely that as you proceed through the evaluation you see interests unfold. This evolving nature of interests must be an integral part of your evaluation. Building in a periodic review of what you see as the important interests can be helpful. Do not expect to define interests at the evaluation's outset and have them be static. You will learn more about interests as the project evolves, so avoid too narrow a definition.

When All Else Fails

Sometimes you encounter a client who is not forthcoming and resists your efforts to open up about purposes. You feel that a shadow agenda

BOX 3-2	Know What Your Client's Interests Are

How to Proceed: Directly ask your client and other stakeholders what the purpose of the evaluation is.

What to Watch Out For: Do not get too narrow a picture of interests.

When All Else Fails: Ask the client's closest confidant what the client wants.

---

exists and that you are being manipulated through withheld information. In such a situation, find the client's closest confidant and informally discuss the situation. This confidant may be the special assistant, a subordinate, an administrative secretary, or a colleague. An informal, low-key discussion that begins with your convincing the confidant that you are after the client's best interests can often yield insights not otherwise available.

KNOW WHAT SUCCESS IS

You and your team should have a clear picture of what defines a successful evaluation. The evaluation's definition of success relates to your client's interests, but it is not the same thing. Typically success in an evaluation incorporates client interests, but success goes beyond just the client's concerns. Success involves specific deliverables, the content of analysis as well as techniques applied, and the interpersonal and political reactions to the evaluation by stakeholders. It also may extend to the rewards you and the team receive from conducting the evaluation. For example, you may take on an evaluation principally to develop programmatic expertise or to enhance your team's applied skills in an analytic methodology. In this case, the actual implementation of the findings may be of secondary concern. Having a picture of success is vital in such cases.

Why is it important to have a clear, specific picture of what a successful conclusion to the evaluation looks like? Because, as the saying goes: "If you don't know where you're going, any road will get you there." A picture of success provides a navigation aid that is essential when you encounter roadblocks. Every evaluation I have ever participated in has had unexpected events crop up. New information, uncooperative interview subjects, and suddenly compressed time deadlines accounted for some of this turbulence. With a clear picture you are prepared to gauge dispassionately such disturbances. This can help you stay on course. It can also help you decide when to change course, if necessary. A clear picture of success facilitates choice and allows you to sort out the exciting from the important.

The Case of the State of Fremont's Drinking Water Program

As a private management consultant I once participated in an evaluation of the drinking water program for the State of Fremont. The client was the director of the program, and the statement of work for the contract called for an evaluation of the effectiveness of the state's drinking water program. My evaluation team members and I were particularly concerned about the vagueness of the work statement. The wording was not so much a deterrent to us as an invitation to explore more carefully the opportunities for work. In preliminary meetings, the evaluation team identified sharpening the definition of success as essential. The drinking water system's performance could be measured in a number of ways: number of enteric disease incidents associated with the system, concentration of various chemicals in customers' blood, or something more process- and efficiency-oriented. We needed to determine the criteria for judgment to develop a real work plan, much less conduct the study. When we met with the director in the entrance interview, it became obvious what success was to the client. He had been under considerable criticism by a number of legislators for the slowness of his staff's review and issuance of permits for developers. Through his body language, direct expression, and general demeanor, we quickly discerned that streamlining the process for review and approval of drinking water system permits was his top interest. When we subsequently described our work plan and the potential range of results, the director strongly validated this interest, and we were able to move forward with little wasted effort. By asking, we could focus the program evaluation on describing the review and approval process and suggest ways to improve the technical soundness of the reviews while speeding them along. Knowing the client's real interest avoided wasting time and produced an evaluation that yielded a happy client as well as additional projects with further billable hours for the consulting firm. It proved to be a win-win situation derived from careful attention to the client's interests.

How to Proceed

At the outset of the project it is important to develop specific descriptions of what the work will produce and the methods you will use to generate the products. And these must be reviewed with the client and the entire project team.

The client must understand and agree to what you will produce, whether it is a report, a briefing, a proposal for further work, and so on. When the work will be completed and the approach you intend to use to do the work are also important. A clear understanding is essential upfront if time is limited. Similarly, if the project methods involve interacting with stakeholders, you may need to factor in political considerations to meet the client's concerns. Being explicit with the client about the timing and the methods can alert you to constraints that are much easier to handle in the design phase instead of the implementation phase of the evaluation.

Your evaluation project staff benefits from a clear delineation of success for the project. When the staff members are on the same page, it is easier to cooperate and work together. When everyone understands what constraints the team faces, unrealistic expectations can be avoided. It is a real danger to an evaluation when the team believes it has one objective and the work emphasizes another. Similarly, if the team plans to use exceptionally sophisticated data collection and analytic techniques, but the project's success does not call for those, then the difference is far easier to manage at the outset instead of as the project rolls out.

What to Watch Out For

Don't become self-employed. Ensure that the definition of success relates back to concerns of the client or the client's stakeholders. Many program evaluations go awry when the conduct of the evaluation itself becomes the team's paramount concern, not the results of the study. Program evaluators at heart are agents acting for principals; they are not the principals. The success of the client governs the evaluation, not the interests of

---

BOX 3-3   **Know What Success Is**

How to Proceed: Develop and share a clear picture of the work products and methods.

What to Watch Out For: Do not become self-employed. Anchor success in the client's interests.

When All Else Fails: Try out two or three success measures on the client and gauge the reaction.

---

the evaluators. Having a clear definition of success and keeping that constantly before everyone involved will avoid heartache.

When All Else Fails

Sometimes you encounter a client who either is not sure what he or she wants or is so guarded that it is impossible to get a clear picture. You know that you have a concern and a client who, in other respects, is worthwhile, but you may not be able to nail down what success is. In such cases it is helpful to try out a few different descriptions of success on the client and gauge the reaction. Typically this would involve describing a project with two or three different success measures and ask the client if that meets his or her needs. When confronted with specificity a client typically reacts in a manner that allows you to know if you are headed in the right direction or not.

HAVE A PRINCIPAL WHO CAN DO SOMETHING

A key feature to understanding your client is knowing whether he or she can do something worthwhile with the study. A primary purpose behind program evaluation is to prompt an organization to improve its operations. This can be extraordinarily difficult without a principal who can move the organization into change. Even with a committed advocate, organizational change normally is not for the faint of heart. Without a committed principal, taking on an evaluation is foolhardy. Consequently, ensure that your client has the capacity, capability, and authority to see that your recommendations get acted upon. Such capacity, capability, and authority are not guarantors of implementation. However, their absence will almost certainly assure that the evaluation stops at the study phase and does not proceed to organizational change. This absence is akin to pushing a rope. You may exert considerable effort, and there may be movement. Such effort and movement, however, do not lead to purposeful accomplishment. Evaluators usually cannot select their clients, but you often can decide whether to take on an assignment or not. One of the key aspects of whether a potential assignment is likely to be successful depends on whether the client can cause something to happen. Assessing a client's interest, capacity, capability, and authority can inform whether you take on an assignment.

The Case of the Shifting Budget Justification

The Prince Edward County Council was beginning its deliberations for the county's annual budget with a major issue concerning the location and construction of a new justice complex. One faction wanted the police headquarters and court building located downtown in Stoneville, the commercial center of the county. Another faction wanted the facility located along a newly constructed bypass. The downtown faction cited the importance of using public investments to stimulate the rejuvenation of downtown; the bypass faction cited the importance of ease of access from the bypass. The previous council had selected the bypass site and, faced with a citizen petition to put the issue to a referendum vote, had delayed committing. This made the decision an election issue, and a new mayor and council were elected on the platform of "doing the public's will" and putting the facility downtown.

As the new council began its first budget deliberations, the members asked the city planner to evaluate the choices. George Harding thus developed an assessment of the pros and cons of each site. He drew on previous studies to assay the costs and benefits and the intangible consequences associated with each site. While doing this, Harding learned that a group of judges had quietly begun to advocate separating the courts and the police headquarters. Harding felt that this decision had already been made. His analysis made no mention of this issue, and he took to the council his evaluation of the (principally) economic consequences to choosing one location over another. These consequences related to the costs of site acquisition, preparation, and building construction. His evaluation was silent on the consequences of stimulating development on the bypass and on the consequences of stimulating development downtown as a result of different siting decisions.

When Harding presented his analysis at the council work session on the budget, it was vigorously attacked by parties on all sides. In one way or another, everyone said that he had omitted consideration of important matters. Harding defended his evaluation by saying that these issues raised intangibles that he could not evaluate, but the council, sensing an opportunity to further defer a contentious decision, expressed strong displeasure with the evaluation and voted to consider retaining an outside consultant to do a "thorough" analysis.

Harding was frustrated, angry, and hurt. He felt he had done a balanced and thorough evaluation and that criticism for leaving out the intangibles was unfair. He felt he had been made a scapegoat by the council because the members did not want to make a decision about the justice complex.

How to Proceed

Deciding whether you have a client who can do something worthwhile or not requires two judgments. First, you have to assess the likely scope of recommendations coming from the study. Second, you have to gauge the power of the client compared with the likely scope of the recommendations. On the one hand, if there is a potential match, or if there looks like there might be a potential match, this can be a signal to proceed. On the other hand, if the potential client's power does not reach what would be necessary to move forward on the possible recommendations, you should gracefully excuse yourself and walk away from the assignment. There is little point in undertaking work that is unlikely to lead to progress.

What to Watch Out For

You are likely to encounter a situation in which a client acknowledges that he or she lacks the power to implement recommendations but nevertheless wishes to proceed with the study as an investment. This is a tough situation. Developing intellectual capital can lead to future change in an

---

BOX 3-4   **Have a Principal Who Can Do Something**

How to Proceed: Decide if your client has the latitude and power to implement findings.

What to Watch Out For: Be careful of doing an evaluation for a client as an investment.

When All Else Fails: Cut your losses and walk away if there is little likelihood of the recommendations being implemented.

---

organization, particularly when this intellectual capital concerns insight into potential profitable changes. You have to decide, not whether the individual has the power to see implementation recommendations carried out, but whether the individual has access to and credibility with those who have such capacity, capability, and influence. In such a situation there is little that can substitute for organizational familiarity. You can get this familiarity through your own experience or through that of those whom you trust. Be careful of undertaking an investment evaluation for a client whom you do not know much about.

When All Else Fails

Sometimes you find yourself in a situation in which the client seems to have the requisite attributes but, as you get into the study, information shows that you were wrong. You cannot stop the study, but you know it is not going to lead to implementation. When you find that the possible changes are outside your client's influence, about the best you can do is to cut your losses: Limit the evaluation's scope. This can be done by turning the study into a fact-based description of the evaluation target and exiting stage left. Do so by providing a product that has utility to the client but does not continue to consume your evaluation resources in pursuit of an outcome that is unlikely to be obtainable.

PUT THE EVALUATION IN A MANAGEMENT CONTEXT

The purpose behind program evaluation is to improve public program effectiveness. This is a core responsibility of management. As a result, you should design and conduct the evaluation to satisfy the question: What must be done to improve performance? Ongoing management of an organization requires constant adaptation of the group's capabilities to the requirements of its environment. Program evaluation is one way of providing information to managers who are making these adjustments. Program evaluation is much more likely to be effective if you do it as a part of an ongoing process of organizational management that seeks to improve organizational behavior within the context of the environmental conditions. This means you must think like a manager: Where do meaningful performance improvement opportunities lie?

The Case of the Executive Assistant's Work Process Study

When Bill Jefferson returned for his second stint as the secretary of a federal government cabinet department, he brought Phil Tomlinson with him to serve as his executive assistant. Tomlinson's job was to review all material and information going to Jefferson. This required Tomlinson to be a gatekeeper for both meetings with the secretary and informational material and paper requiring the secretary's signature. Tomlinson controlled access to Jefferson, whether personally or in writing. Given that about fifteen thousand people worked in the department and many issues were highly controversial, a substantial demand was put on Jefferson's time. Tomlinson arbitrated and allocated the scarce resource of access to the secretary.

Tomlinson requested an evaluation of his activities. He was overwhelmed with the workload and believed changes were needed in how the executive level of the department made decisions. While not a classic program evaluation, the problem came to the program evaluation division. It undertook the project after meeting with Tomlinson at his request. He was clearly motivated to change; his performance had substantial impact on the rest of the department; and he had the authority from the secretary to rearrange operating processes. The project was fairly straightforward but not simple. The team characterized the decision-making and information-handling processes in the secretary's suite, identified the major problems, and recommended alterations. Tomlinson altered responsibilities and, to some degree, behaviors, which led to faster information flow and less direct work for him. By viewing improvement as a management activity, the evaluation team in a few weeks was able to develop proposals that were gratefully embraced by a drowning senior political executive.

A collateral consequence of this was that Tomlinson felt well served by the team and recommended the division be used by others at the political level of the department. This produced a series of engagements in program evaluation that ran the gamut of program and administrative management. In essence, applying a management perspective on a program evaluation led to considerable additional assignments concerning important program performance issues that previously the division had not been involved in.

How to Proceed

At the outset of the evaluation, in fact, before you agree to undertake the work, you must clearly define the purpose of the program to be evaluated and consider your potential to contribute to advancing the program's purpose. Sometimes you may not be able to clearly describe the program's purpose. This, in itself, should be a red flag for you. Perhaps you could undertake an evaluation and contribute to the program by helping sharpen its purpose. Or perhaps it is likely to be a hopeless endeavor. You must assess that based on your judgment of the situation. But this assessment must be grounded in the question: What must be done to improve performance from the management perspective?

What to Watch Out For

Conflicting objectives can cause real problems. But all public programs have multiple objectives. It is important to assess whether the objectives are complementary, competitive, or contradictory. Are the objectives sufficiently clear and noncontradictory to permit a reasoned opportunity for improvement? If so, jumping in may be well worth considering. If not, such a situation should raise a cautionary flag before you decide to proceed.

When All Else Fails

In your project-scoping meeting with the client and related staff, ask: What is the first thing that should be done in the program? This will force the client to spell out management priorities and can yield insight into

BOX 3-5	Put the Evaluation in a Management Context

How to Proceed: Conduct the work with program improvement as the core objective.

What to Watch Out For: Beware of conflicting objectives.

When All Else Fails: Ask the client what the program needs to improve first.

---

the management opportunities that could exist. You may get different answers based on the various organizational levels represented or the role of individual stakeholders. However, it should be fairly easy to judge when you face an opportunity for improvement and when you face an impossible situation.

DO THE RIGHT THING

Your first obligation to the client as well as to yourself, your colleagues, and your profession is to conduct the evaluation so that you uphold contemporary standards of ethics. If you do everything else correctly, but suffer a lapse in ethical conduct during the evaluation, all of your good work will be washed away. You must do the right thing as you see it to preserve the integrity of the analysis and your own self-worth. If ethical principles are violated, this will place into doubt all basic conduct and conclusions. In short, if you cannot be trusted to uphold basic ethical values, there is little chance your descriptive characterizations, analytic understandings, and recommended actions can be trusted.

The Case of 'Let's Not Use This Data'

During the mid-1970s, some of the most highly sought-after development land in the Baintree metropolitan area was placed off limits to development because of lack of sewage treatment capacity. An integral piece of this decision concerned disposal of sludge from wastewater treatment in the region. If economic growth was to proceed, the sludge disposal problem had to be solved. Composting sludge to transform it from a valueless residual to a valuable product was identified as a possible way to meet the challenge. The major issue concerned whether the composting process would kill the nasty pathogens in the sludge. The local sewage agency undertook studies to assess the viability of composting. Initial tests indicated pathogen destruction occurred by the heat generated in the composting process. A great exultation among politicians and developers ensued. The commission's managers were applauded as saviors of economic progress. When larger scale test results arrived, however, the optimistic results of the first test were not supported. It did not look like composting would work after all. During staff meetings to examine the results, a manager suggested, "Let's not use these results. We have the earlier ones that were good, so that's all we need." The engineer who had been charged with evaluating the program objected. He asserted that he would resign if the second results were discarded. The manager quickly backed down, and the compromise of conducting a second set of studies was agreed to. Those studies did not show a pathogen problem and, in fact, uncovered a flaw in the test method that yielded the problematic results. By threatening to resign, the evaluator forced further data collection that provided a much sounder footing for action and avoided the unethical proposal that the pressured manager had advanced.

How to Proceed

There is a simple test to use concerning ethicality of a position. Ask yourself if you would want your action summarized on a billboard outside your office. If your answer is no, then you need to look for a different action than the one you were contemplating.

What to Watch Out For

Be careful of two threats. First, beware of sanctimoniousness. It is unusual for people to actively choose to do what they view as a wrong thing. People have reasons for what they do, and those reasons may be good or not so good. Regardless, a sure sign that you have not fully considered the competing ethical aspects of a situation is when you feel self-righteous.

Second, beware of becoming an apologist for unacceptable behavior. This is especially likely when you are dealing with a client who is particularly attractive. This attractiveness may stem from power, personal charm,

BOX 3-6	Do the Right Thing

How to Proceed: Ask yourself if you would mind having your actions announced on a billboard outside your office.

What to Watch Out For: Beware of becoming sanctimonious or an apologist.

When All Else Fails: Walk away, explain why to the client, and document your reasons privately.

---

or policy preferences you support. For whatever reason, you must maintain professional detachment and guard against adopting the preferences of your client over what you know to be ethical behavior.

When All Else Fails

Be willing to walk away from the evaluation and make clear, privately, why you are doing so. Prepare a written explanation, share it with your client, and keep a copy in a safe place. Depending upon the subsequent circumstances, you may have to widen the circle of those who know what happened and why. This may involve people for whom you work, legislators, or the press. Whether and which ones depend on the circumstances. It is important to prepare a documented explanation at the time events were unfolding. This will likely be more accurate because the facts are fresh in your mind, and it will also establish the legitimacy of your intentions.

EXERCISES AND DISCUSSION QUESTIONS

1. Select a public program and identify those who might have a direct interest in it. Discuss why or why not each party would support evaluation of this program.

2. Why is it important to understand the definition of success for a program evaluation from the client's viewpoint?

3. You have undertaken a program evaluation for a client who is the manager of a program in a nonprofit organization. During the data

collection phase you learn confidentially that the client has been told he will be released by the organization's board. How could that affect your evaluation? What might you do in response?

4. What are the pros and cons of separating program evaluation from management? If it were done, what could be the best way to do so? What would be the likely adverse effects of the separation?

5. During the course of evaluating a local government program in a council-manager form of government, the council election produces a dramatic shift in the ideological alignment of the council. How should you proceed? Would your action depend on the nature of the ideological shift or would it be independent of ideology? What conditions could affect your decision?

6. What do you believe is the single most important principle to observe in interacting with a client of a program evaluation? Why?

7. When a program evaluation has multiple clients, how would you approach client relations when their interests conflict with one another?

8. In the case of the open space program, assume you represent the developer who wishes to justify using open space bonds to construct the sidewalks and parking lots. What type of research would you undertake to identify supporting ideas for this position? If you were retained by the Collegeville Open Space and Trails Commission, what type of research would you conduct to counter such analyses?

9. In the case of the shifting budget justification, what would you have done differently from George Harding? Once the council chose to bring in an outside consultant, what conditions and assumptions would you place on the engagement if you were the outside consultant?

4

KNOW THE CONTENT

Program evaluation examines real conditions and compares them with intended consequences. More specifically, it uses rational processes to examine the conduct of a program and assess its characteristics and effectiveness along with the sources of these qualities. To do this, we must constantly ask ourselves how we can be reasonably certain that the information collection and analysis processes we follow will yield valid insights. In short, we must know the actual content of the program to do our job.

A wealth of good books have been published on the technical conduct of program evaluations. These concern themselves with the design, data collection, analysis, and communication of program evaluations. These books share the assumption that precision of understanding and strength of persuasiveness in program evaluations depend upon the reliability and specificity of analysis and argument. If evaluators want to gain insight and persuade others of the need to act to improve programs, they need to base their case upon empirical evidence. The books are excellent sources for the application of nuanced approaches. But every one of them starts with the fundamental premise that sound program evaluation research must yield specific and reliable empirical evidence. To do this, evaluators need to know the content of the program they are evaluating. Concepts are important; without them program evaluation risks terminal extemporaneity. But whatever is done has to start with actual conditions, and these conditions are the real content of the program. Who does what; when they

---

BOX 4-1   The Content Practices

Build the Analysis on Facts

Align Your Evidence and Your Conclusions

Simplicity Always Trumps Elegance

Don't Let the Illusion of the Perfect Drive Out the Reality of the Good

Never Underestimate the Power of Accurate Description

---

do it; where their venues are; and how the processes are carried out can yield insight. As Rudyard Kipling wrote in "The Elephant's Child":

> *I keep six honest serving-men*
> *(They taught me all I knew);*
> *Their names are What and Why and When*
> *And How and Where and Who.*[1]

There is no substitute for knowing what you are doing. This means, first, having a specific, reliable understanding of the program. Second, it means analyzing your data employing appropriate and insightful techniques. But the recipe for duck soup always starts with: "First, get a duck." So start with knowing the content of the program you are evaluating.

BUILD THE ANALYSIS ON FACTS

The core of program evaluation must come from the actual characteristics of the situation. Everyone involved with the program—the client, the program implementers, the program's clients, and other stakeholders—are interested in the facts of the program. Intentions aside, what happens determines the program's success and opportunities for improvement. A fact profile can provide the foundation for an evaluation. Sometimes simply by arraying the facts a program evaluation can advance improvement by providing a common understanding of the actual conditions. Not only must this fact profile be based on actual conditions, but these conditions also must be a valid characterization of the situation. So, we must pay careful attention to getting basic, accurate, and reliable facts.

Which facts should we focus on? Frequently when an evaluator collects data about a program under study, a large amount of information piles up. How can he or she identify the information that truly matters to the evaluation and the rest that, if not unimportant, at least is likely to be less important than other data? Sort through extensive data using the purpose of the program as a guide. Look to see if the information can be grouped, or bundled, together by category, then prioritize the data in order of what you believe might be relevant to the purpose of the program. You may be right or you may be wrong, but start with data that seem most relevant to the program's outcome then move through information in ever-decreasing likely importance to program impact. As you learn about some data's usefulness, you may confirm your prioritization, or you may find that your initial ranking should be revised. But starting with a guess at outcome impacts can help you sort through large and varied amounts of data.

The Case of Virginia's Mental Health Program

The value of accurate characterization of a program's basic facts is illustrated by a program evaluation conducted of the State of Virginia's mental health deinstitutionalization efforts.[2] The Virginia Joint Legislative and Audit Review Commission evaluated the delivery of mental health services provided by state and local governments. It examined the number of patients, local and state service providers, and records to create a profile of the existing program delivering mental health services outside of traditional mental health institutions. Its case studies, interviews, and surveys of mental health clients produced a characterization of the size of the client pool and the description of the process of services delivery as well as the distribution of responsibilities of the service providers. These characterizations identified underfunding and lack of administrative control as key areas that required action to improve the mental health system. The coherent characterization of the facts resulted in recommendations to improve the program. The evaluators built their analysis on facts, and those facts, without elaborate causal analysis, led to improvement.

How to Proceed

Start with the facts of the program. Look for the basic characteristics of the program. Do they shed light on the size of the problem under consideration, the interests that are in play, and the processes that are used? If you have a large amount of different data, go after those that seem most closely related to program objectives. Descriptive statistics such as range, mean, median, and mode can be of great help getting a picture of the overall program.[3] Total quality management analytic tools such as process flow charts, Ishikawa diagrams, and force-field analysis yield insight into the nature of the work and where problems may be cropping up.[4]

It is typically helpful to begin with Kipling's six honest serving-men for any program and then move to describing the work process flows. These characterizations may often reveal program features that have been overlooked and can lead to improvement. There is great advantage to straightforward depictions of what is going on. You will likely encounter many folks who believe they know what is happening. However, this knowledge may be based on supposition or on what they believe ought to be occurring instead of what is truly happening on the ground. I have found that what everyone knows is often what they hope or believe, and it can be unrelated to what is actually going on. In such cases a little factual analysis can help you understand the actual conditions. And surprising insights may occur.

What to Watch Out For

Be careful of selecting your facts to match a predetermined problem analysis or policy outcome. You need to see conditions as closely to reality as you can. Sound data collection techniques are absolutely essential here.[5] Make sure that what you are seeing is representative of the actual situation and not a misleading subset. Bias is the great danger here. Accuracy is your ally. A skeptical mind can be a helpful friend, and a closed mind heightens the peril of doing a program evaluation.

When All Else Fails

Make a list of what you know and what you do not know about the program. Figure 4-1 is one template to follow. List the characteristics, where the information about them came from, and why you believe the characteristics are important. Next list the holes in your knowledge about the program. For each element show why you think it is important and where you would have to get the missing information. Summarize why

FIGURE 4-1	**Program Characteristics Table Sample**

PROGRAM COMPONENT	Description	Information source	Why relevant	Notes
Stakeholders				
Clients				
Advocates				
Opponents				
Collateral interests				
Operational features				
Annual budget				
Annual staffing				
Sources of funding				
Measures of success				
Legal basis				
Municipal ordinance				
State statutes				
Federal laws				
Recent changes				

you do not have this information. When you are finished, ask yourself if what you have is adequate to move forward, and, if so, how you would proceed. If it is inadequate, list what you need to do to make up the deficiency. If you do not have the facts, you do not have the basis for an informed evaluation.

ALIGN YOUR EVIDENCE AND YOUR CONCLUSIONS

Clients hire program evaluators to examine programs. While they may do so for a range of reasons, the most prevalent concerns gaining insight not

BOX 4-2	Build the Analysis on Facts

How to Proceed: Summarize the basic facts that describe the program.

What to Watch Out For: Beware of selecting facts to match a predetermined analysis or policy outcome.

When All Else Fails: Make a table of what you know and do not know about the program.

---

otherwise available. In other words, evaluators' value added often comes from independently and reliably describing programs and reaching conclusions based on the depictions. In doing this, your conclusions about the program must be drawn from specific evidence. Assertion without evidence is unconvincing.

For program improvement to occur, someone other than the evaluator must act. Convincing people to act requires evidence that aligns with conclusions. Without evidence to support your conclusions, the only thing you are left with is uninformed prejudice. Most clients and stakeholders can easily ferret out snow jobs. They reached their positions of responsibility based on some capacity to detect authentic, valid information and to act on it. Evidence is the essential ingredient, and with evidence you can formulate a foundation for program improvement.

The Case of a Critical Transportation Project

An evaluation based on facts can produce a change in behavior for a project or a program. A major highway between the cities of Collegeville and Downing in the State of Fremont was slated for widening. The road crossed a river about halfway between the two cities. The river was the backbone of a wildlife corridor within these rapidly urbanizing areas. The corridor presented the most significant open space in a region of one million people.

The State of Fremont's Department of Transportation (DOT) proposed to replace the existing bridge as part of the highway expansion. However, the proposed bridge's length would choke wildlife use of the corridor because of its narrowness. Local citizen groups mobilized and persuaded the DOT to lengthen the bridge to enhance the corridor. They had gathered facts about the additional cost, the prior and projected future local government capital investments that were threatened, the established practice elsewhere to provide for wildlife corridors, and the range of local government and nongovernment interests that were deeply concerned about the length of the bridge. While not a classic program evaluation, this situation demonstrates the value of basing arguments upon facts. The proposed bridge subsequently was deemed too short. Evidence of an economic, environmental, and political nature was marshaled to support that position. In this case, evidence and conclusions were aligned and project improvement occurred as a result.

How to Proceed

For every conclusion you reach, aim for having three actual conditions that support the conclusion. If you offer one example, those opposing your view will say, "You've got only one example that supports your view. We can't act on just one data point." If you offer two examples, people will say, "OK, but you've exhausted your arguments." With three examples, opponents will believe you have a wealth of arguments that you can throw into the discussion and, consequently, will likely accept your conclusion.

What to Watch Out For

Be certain that what you have observed is valid. Do not reach a conclusion with one or no facts. If you have a single fact, view that as encouragement to look further, not to close on a recommendation. Watch for adopting a recommendation that lacks evidence. You probably are wondering how that can happen. Often recommendations get packaged together. For example, there may be support for one recommendation, but factual support for the other may not be there. In such cases the validity for one covers for invalidity of the other. It is sort of like one person paying for admission to a nightclub, but two people slipping past the velvet rope together. It is wrong, it is obvious, but it happens. Do not let that happen with your recommendations. Ensure that each recommendation rises or falls on its own merit and factual justification, not simply the validity of its nearby cousin. You may get an unsubstantiated recommen-

---

BOX 4-3   **Align Your Evidence and Your Conclusions**

How to Proceed: Have three conditions that support each conclusion you reach.

What to Watch Out For: Be sure you do not reach a conclusion based on supposition, not facts, because it is what you want.

When All Else Fails: Get another member of your team to verify that your facts support your conclusions.

---

dation past some, but the chances of successfully slipping it past everyone is nil. Trying to do that will get you in big trouble.

When All Else Fails

Do not reach a conclusion or make a recommendation without factual evidence, however broadly you might construe it. A helpful way to snake check a recommendation is to get another member of the team who is knowledgeable but not invested in the conclusion to look at the recommendation and the evidence. He or she can tell you whether the recommendation passes the laugh test. If it does not, you should be prepared to say "I don't know" when pressed for a recommendation under such conditions. It is far better to commit a sin of omission than a sin of commission. In more formal terms, do not reject the null hypothesis without adequate evidence.

SIMPLICITY ALWAYS TRUMPS ELEGANCE

A great temptation exists in program evaluation to use the most sophisticated analytic technique available. In part this is due to the desire to exercise skills that have been developed at great cost and energy. If someone is going to go to the trouble to learn logistic regression, for example, it is human nature to want to use it. Furthermore, sophisticated analytic techniques, especially those employing statistics, can yield nuanced and precise understandings unavailable through other means. But using these techniques requires that a trade-off always be considered: the value added through the insight derived from using the techniques versus the transaction costs of explaining it to those less familiar with such techniques. Sophisticated analysis yields insight, but at a price. In many circumstances we are better off using the least sophisticated analytic tool that gets the job done, even if it means sacrificing some precision of insight.

There is a good reason for evaluators to have a bias toward least analytic force. A characterization that is simpler is easier to understand. If a client can understand something, he or she is more likely to be able to engage the substance that the analytic force concerns. When a client has to expend intellectual energy processing information, such as understanding advanced analytic techniques and their limitations, he or she has less intellectual energy to consider the substance revealed by the analytic technique. Simple and understandable characterizations typically are more convincing than mathematically complex interpretations. Executives usually are not familiar with modeling details; they are more comfortable using their informed judgment. The key challenge for the evaluator is to provide the informed part so that the information can be absorbed by the client. It does no good to impress the client with your command of structural equation modeling, for example, if he or she does not understand the findings and either ignores the information or, perhaps worse, misunderstands the analysis and reaches incorrect conclusions.

The Case of the Incineration at Sea Program Proposal

The value of simple characterization in an analysis occurred during an evaluation of the program to advocate incinerating hazardous wastes on sea-borne vessels. The disposal of hazardous wastes is technically difficult, costly, and politically difficult. This last feature derives from the Not In My Backyard (NIMBY) syndrome: No one wants wastes near his or her neighborhood. A way around the NIMBY problem was advanced in the early 1980s, which was to build state-of-the-art hazardous wastes incinerators on ships, load the wastes onto the vessels, sail them to international waters where there are no backyards, and incinerate them there.

A pilot test burn had been conducted that showed such combustion operations would render the wastes inert. An evaluation of the program was sought, and the environmental analysis division of the State of Fremont's Department of Environmental Quality examined the program. By simple mathematics, the team demonstrated that the number of ships required to incinerate the hazardous wastes would be staggering. When that insight was combined with the number of loading facilities that would be required to handle the waste, the national policy makers concluded that incineration at sea was impractical. No complex modeling of the waste streams was necessary, although the modeling was readily available. A simple calculation of the future capacity required demonstrated the infeasible nature of the incineration at sea program. A straightforward description of the volume of waste and the facilities required to incinerate the waste brought everyone to conclude the approach would not work.

How to Proceed

Sophisticated modeling can yield insight, but be sure that you need the modeling to achieve your desired result, that is, empirical insight into the actual situation. Regression analysis in its varied forms, principal components analysis, and structural equation modeling are valuable, but before they are employed be certain you need the precision in understanding that they provide. They, and their analytic cousins, should be used only when necessary to probe a complex situation for nuanced insights. They should never be used to dazzle the client. The dazzle will likely confuse and alienate the client at the cost of loss of understanding. In such a situation, you default upon your first obligation as an evaluator—to provide information that reliably assists in improvement.

What to Watch Out For

Do not get so enamored with mathematical sophistication that you forget that insight and persuasion are your objective, not demonstrating your command of econometrics or other nifty analytic techniques.

When All Else Fails

Your bias should be for the simple and logical over the complex and logical. You are more likely to communicate important information more clearly under such conditions. Go to complex analytic techniques only when you are satisfied that it is necessary to yield insight for improving the program. Simplicity always trumps elegance, all other things equal. Never exert more analytic force than you need to get the job done. No one likes or listens to a show-off.

BOX 4-4	Simplicity Always Trumps Elegance

How to Proceed: Use the minimum level of analysis necessary to demonstrate your point.

What to Watch Out For: Do not become so dazzled with mathematical rigor that you overlook simple analytic insights.

When All Else Fails: Prefer the simple and logical over the complex and logical.

DON'T LET THE ILLUSION OF THE PERFECT DRIVE OUT THE REALITY OF THE GOOD

One invaluable characteristic of many well-educated people is the ability to envision a situation that is substantially different and better than what exists. Such an ability enables improvement because it provides direction and purpose to program evaluations. However, too much of a good thing can be a bad thing. It is easy to imagine a perfect solution to a problem identified in an evaluation, while pursuit of that perfect solution can lead to the rejection of a workable and real solution.

This problem derives from two fallacies that you must constantly be alert to in considering the content of a program evaluation. First, the fascination with the perfect is fascination with something that does not exist and will likely never exist. Real situations have limits, discontinuities, and unexpected results. All of these can be conveniently overlooked as we imagine a perfect solution. In the actual world of program execution these qualities cannot be overlooked. Sometimes they even become the predominant concern. So focusing on a perfect solution is focusing on the nonexistent. Wasting energy doing this diverts energy from other more profitable efforts.

The second fallacy is that perfection is so important because you have only one chance to achieve it. In this view, evaluation and the management it supports are single-shot enterprises: Act, then move on to something else, leaving the program in the past. This is simply not how evaluations and management function. Constant, recursive attention to operations and results is the principal foundation of effective management.[6] To obtain effective results with an evaluation, you must take this into account.

Some evaluations are, in fact, single-shot efforts. In such cases the probability for improvement is reduced. Ongoing attention to outcomes is absent. However, it is well worth the risk to set aside the chimera that a perfect program can be realized in favor of a second-best approach that avoids the fallacy of single-shot improvement.

The Case of the Coke Ovens Emissions

The Environmental Protection Agency was charged under the Clean Air Act with regulating the emissions of benzene from coke ovens. Benzene is a known carcinogen for humans. The level of control depends upon how often workers patrolled the coke ovens to inspect for visible leaks of gas coming out of the lids and doors and to seal the leaks they observed. The policy question regarding setting a regulatory control level was about how intensive the patrols would need to be.

The agency engaged in extensive engineering and economic analyses to select the emissions control level. The debate focused on two options: a 95 percent control level and a 98 percent control level. The first option was slightly cheaper, with the policy debate raging over whether the health effects warranted the 98 percent level. All the while this was going on, the coke ovens had essentially 0 percent controls. So, for eighteen months the evaluation debate was about a difference of 3 percent, during which time no controls at all were being applied. Eventually the 95 percent level was selected by the administrator, but that was challenged in court by outside interest groups.

An interesting aside was that the technique used to control the oven emissions called for a worker to insert caulk in the lid or door where the leak was observed and use a sledgehammer to seal the leak. Even if the perfect solution had been found, implementation required using extremely crude tools. In this case, the perfect was the enemy of the good, with the result being that the public was exposed to uncontrolled emissions for eighteen months while debate raged over what could reasonably be determined as nonexistent.

BOX 4-5	Don't Let the Illusion of the Perfect Drive Out the Reality of the Good

How to Proceed: Ask yourself if the anticipated improvement can be achieved under the conditions likely to exist over the next five years.

What to Watch Out For: Do not let the perfect become the enemy of the good.

When All Else Fails: Get a second opinion about the perfect versus good trade-offs you are considering.

How to Proceed

When faced with a range of possible improvements in an evaluation, ask yourself if the promised improvement is likely to be achievable under the conditions that will exist over the next three to five years. If not, look to the next best alternative. If so, you need to scrutinize the alternative closely. Always remember that there is rarely such a thing as a permanent fix to any problem in the public sector. If the solution is practicable in the foreseeable future, go for it. If the solution requires an infinite time horizon for it to be worthwhile, start looking for another alternative.

What to Watch Out For

Remember that the perfect can become the enemy of the good. Just because you can describe a unicorn does not mean it exists. Do not allow your ability to imagine a better result lure you into rejecting a good outcome unless the chances for better improvements are quite high.

When All Else Fails

If you feel uncertain about which route to take, ask someone whose judgment you trust and who is unfamiliar with the project to give you a second opinion about the possible trade-offs. If another smart person says it looks suspect, it just might be suspect. Remember the first rule of public service: "First, don't do anything stupid."

NEVER UNDERESTIMATE THE POWER OF ACCURATE DESCRIPTION

Often a program evaluation can be successful by organizing information that is readily available. This depends upon important insights hiding in plain sight. The complications and confusing information that characterize most public programs can obscure key facts. In such conditions, the program evaluation provides great value by clearing away the mostly irrelevant underbrush and displaying the pertinent for people to see. A clear and comprehensive description of a situation can often lead to insightful problem analysis and solution selection.

There is a good reason that accurate description can lead to a valuable program evaluation. Day-to-day program management operations often involve so much fog that characterization organized around the interests of a principal can reveal previously masked solutions. Attending to the personal petitions, the incomplete and sometimes irrelevant information, and the conflicting objectives typical of routine public program management can obscure what is important. Your program evaluation can help by removing the obstacles. By looking at the program from a viewpoint external to the operations, you may be able to identify the forest from the trees. While conceptually simple, this requires sharpened senses of perception and judgment of what is and is not important to the program as well as the talent to display such information so that the obvious is revealed.

The Case of Answering Congressional Inquiries

In federal government agencies, responsiveness to members of Congress is highly valued. Legislators control both purse strings and authorizing legislation for the agencies, so direct interaction with a member gets high priority. One of the most frequent interactions concerns letters sent to the agencies by the members on behalf of a constituent. These inquiries may range from seeking help with obtaining passports, getting a child transferred from one military duty station to another, or finding out the status of a regulation important to a business in the member's district. Whatever the topic, the agencies almost always closely track each query to ensure that a timely answer is provided. Getting quick responses to these "congressionals" is a big deal.

One cabinet-level agency's regional office was having difficulty getting these letters back to the members within two weeks, the processing time set by the D.C. headquarters. An internal consulting group evaluated the regional office's process for assigning the work to answer the congressionals. The first task was to spell out the steps for answering the letters. When the program evaluation team sought to do this, it found that there was not one process in the region, but multiple processes. Which process was followed depended upon which secretary handled the initial paperwork. And often the process was changed in midstream if a different secretary picked up the job of tracking the letter. Simply by seeking to describe the process, the team identified the need for the regional office to settle on a single, clear, understandable process as the primary requirement to improve carrying out this task. The streamlining that occurred when multiple, overlapping processes were replaced with a single process won praise from those in the office who were tired of getting criticized for missing key deadlines. And it enabled the office to cut the number of late responses dramatically. This was achieved through describing a process that everyone thought he or she knew.

How to Proceed

Whenever you begin a program evaluation, make the first step a description of the program and the processes involved. Two things will flow from this. First, you deepen your understanding of what the real work of the program is. And second, you may find that the description uncovers disconnects that can yield big improvements quickly.

What to Watch Out For

Beware of getting mired in details. You can easily accumulate so many descriptive details that you lose track of basic concerns. This work is not simply reportorial; it requires analysis, judgment, and interpretation to focus on the important features. This may look like a descriptive task, but to do so with value-added requires you to think analytically while you are describing the program and its processes.

When All Else Fails

Make a list of everything you know about the program that you believe affects the program outcome. Rank these in order of importance as you define importance at that time, then take the first one and ask if the description you have is likely to be accurate and whether a different

BOX 4-6	Never Underestimate the Power of Accurate Description

How to Proceed: Make the first step in the evaluation a description of the important features of the program.

What to Watch Out For: Avoid getting mired in details.

When All Else Fails: List and rank everything in the program that affects the outcome, then ask if each one were different would the result be substantially different.

---

description would materially impact the program's outcome. Go after those that look fuzzy and are important simultaneously.

EXERCISES AND DISCUSSION QUESTIONS

1. Identify a decision made recently by your state legislature about a significant program. Array the key facts relating to this decision. Identify which ones were known prior to enactment. How did the knowledge of the facts, or the lack of knowledge, influence the legislative decision?

2. For a particular program choice recently featured in the national news, develop three arguments for the decision that employ facts. Do the same for arguments against the decision. Which are most persuasive and why?

3. Many public programs are extremely complex and nuanced. They may impact different groups in varied ways. What are the dangers of using a simplicity-trumps-elegance approach in such settings? How would you approach such situations to improve a program's effectiveness?

4. Identify a recent controversial land use or zoning decision in your city. What were the factors that argued for changing the zoning or proposal? What were the factors that argued against the change?

5. Ask the staff of the registrar's office of your university to list the steps necessary to secure graduation approval. Ask the staff of your

academic department the same question. Are they the same? If they differ, why?

6. As a program evaluator you have learned in the course of a project that a unit you have become familiar with will be abolished. Some of the staff, with whom you have become friends, likely will be laid off. There are openings in a firm in the area that call for skills like those of the staffers who are expected to lose their jobs. But the application dates for those jobs close prior to announcement of the abolition of the unit. Would you alert your friends and violate a professional confidence or remain silent and allow your friends to be hurt? Why? What would be the arguments for the other position?

7. In the case of the benzene coke ovens emissions, what tactics would you have recommended to break the decision-making logjam? What is the relationship between analytic content and political interests that could have affected the outcome?

8. In the case of the Virginia mental health program, a major conclusion concerned inadequacy of funding. Many public programs typically are underfunded. Assume that you were an evaluator presenting the findings to a legislative committee. In the course of your presentation, a committee member accuses you of providing information that is predictable and unhelpful. What type of information would you want to have at your elbow to counter this criticism?

5

CONTROL THE WORK

Program evaluation is real work. By "real work" I mean that it involves strenuous effort, often by a number of people oriented to achieving some outcome, with everyone adding value to each other's contributions. The evaluation may have lofty goals such as improving delivery of public services. However, these goals cannot be achieved unless real work gets done. And how this work gets done determines the timeliness, cost, and quality of the evaluation. Seeing that everyone knows his or her job, knows when to contribute, and knows how his or her work fits with other team members' makes up the essence of how work for the evaluation project is controlled. Controlling this real work can make the difference between a successful program evaluation and one whose intention is praiseworthy but whose execution leaves clients dissatisfied.

Program evaluation seeks evidence-based insight into public program performance and improvement, but it shares with most other projects the need for clarity of expectations and accountability to deliver the goods. If evaluators hope to get results that can lead to improving a program, they need to control the often-complicated individual and team efforts that go into a program evaluation. Intentions do not yield improvements; results do. Getting those results usually requires sound project management. Focusing on managing the project features of the program evaluation can help bring about a successful evaluation. To do this, start with a coherent and usable work plan.

BOX 5-1   **The Control Practices**

Have a Real Work Plan

Meet the Deadline

Getting People with the Right Skills and Temperament

Expect Something to Go Wrong

Use More Than One Set of Eyes

Know Your Core Values

HAVE A REAL WORK PLAN

A work plan provides an effective way to identify and monitor what is necessary to complete and deliver the evaluation. It stipulates who will deliver what and when. It provides two valuable contributions to a program evaluation. First, it lays out in a coherent manner the complete set of activities needed to do the work. It thus provides a check on the completeness of the work activities, and it establishes responsibilities for staff. People perform better if they own a piece of work, and a work plan tells everyone who is on the hook for what. Second, it provides a way to monitor whether the work is getting done. Program evaluators are professionals, but they are people, too. If left without adequate monitoring and feedback, they may not meet the expectations associated with project success. Project drift occurs when objectives and methods change under the pressure of day-to-day conditions. The antidote to project drift is constant reference to the work plan.

Most program evaluations involve myriad activities carried out by multiple analysts. These analysts usually are smart, energetic, and independent. All of these are qualities essential for successful knowledge workers. However, they often can interfere with work being done in groups. That is where a work plan comes in handy. It helps avoid project drift or analyst self-employment in a setting in which cooperative effort is essential. It keeps everyone sitting on his or her horse facing the end with the ears.

For a project's work plan to help evaluators do their job, it must have a number of characteristics. It must be complete; no important activities should be overlooked. It must be specific; products to be delivered and the timing of that delivery must be clear. It must connect actual humans on the evaluation team with the activities and products; names should be tied to obligations. And it must be usable. This means it must be both understandable and updated as conditions change. It is a working document, with the emphasis on "working."

Another helpful aspect of a work plan is its use in flagging problems. Work falling off schedule can indicate substantive as well as management problems. A work plan can serve as a useful early warning device during the conduct of the evaluation.

The Case of Matrix Management in the Program Evaluation Division

At one point our management team found the program evaluation division facing more projects than could be done given its traditional management approach of separate line organizations. The team members and I found ourselves having to shift people from different units to work on multiple projects, some of which were in their organizational home and some of which were not. We decided to adopt a matrix management approach in which each project was executed by a team drawn from skills across organizational units and led by a project manager.

To keep up with the various staffing demands as well as the multiple project deliverables, we found that requiring a project work plan helped keep straight who was doing what. We were driven to do this to avoid resource overcommitments and to keep track of the many reports, briefings, and interviews that were the responsibility of each team. But what we also found was that using a work plan imposed considerable discipline on the methodology used in each project. Previously we were able to leave project specifics vague because the particular line organization could sharpen the methodology as needed while the project developed. When we had to describe each project's conduct with specificity about activities, timing, and staffing, we found we had to think more clearly about the methodology being used. This injected additional rigor in our work that we had not expected and which improved the quality of the evaluations. The work plan diminished the extemporaneity of previous work and not

FIGURE 5-1   **Example Work Plans**

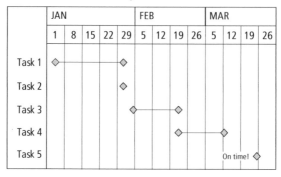

Project Title

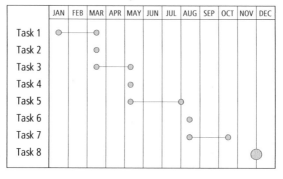

Project Title

only strengthened the conduct of the work but also provided the staff clarity about expectations for their performance.

How to Proceed

Use a simple method to keep track of the key features of an evaluation project: activity, delivery, timing, and staff responsibility. Figure 5-1 illustrates some useful formats, but you can make up your own. Just ensure that you get the basic components in front of you and your staff in a manner that is fairly easy to understand and does not require huge resources to keep current.

BOX 5-2	Have a Real Work Plan

How to Proceed: Devise a method to keep track of the key features of the project: activity, delivery, timing, and staff responsibility.

What to Watch Out For: Do not draw up a work plan that is so information-hungry that it takes more effort to produce than it yields.

When All Else Fails: Review each evaluation project or subproject weekly with staff and managers.

What to Watch Out For

Do not overcomplicate project work plans. These things can gobble up resources. Many available software packages are extremely detailed, so much so few use them because they require too much effort. Stay away from something that does not pass the use test: Ask yourself if you can put the work plan into action without disrupting staffing patterns to provide the raw information. If you are not sure, stop. Take a closer look and see if you can simplify things. If something looks complicated in design, it almost certainly will be overly complicated in implementation. These things grow, so make allowances and employ the simplest method possible.

When All Else Fails

Every week look at all evaluation projects one by one. Have the project team identify each task to be done for the upcoming week and who will do it. Then meet with either the project manager or the entire team to discuss the schedule, the products, and the problems that are showing up.

MEET THE DEADLINE

The world is full of people who overpromise and underdeliver. Do not be one of those. Reliability builds trust, and trust is essential for a principal to act on program evaluation findings and recommendations. Within reasonable bounds, you must deliver the evaluation work on schedule and within budget or ahead of time and at less cost than promised.

Principals usually believe that not getting the evaluation done on time is a signal of a general low-quality product. These people have extraordinary claims upon their time, and the problems they are asked to solve are ones no one else can fix. Anything that is well done and timely has a positive cachet: It makes their life easier. It will give you a huge advantage in the persuasion department if you are routinely able to bring an evaluation project in on time and on budget.

You can meet the deadline through a number of strategies. First, you can accurately estimate the time it will take to do the work. Having a specific and knowledgeable understanding of the methodology of the evaluation is essential. Second, you can build in a cushion of time in the schedule. If you believe the work will take twelve weeks, you might provide thirteen weeks on the schedule. You then will have some resiliency to absorb unexpected overages in production time. Third, you can closely monitor work performance to identify very early any threats that might arise. It is much easier to correct a problem and diminish its impact if you can start working on it as soon as it occurs instead of allowing a considerable time to elapse before acting. Lastly, you can extemporize when a problem arises. This is a dangerous strategy to use as anything other than a last resort. The reason is obvious: You may not be able to create a solution and are left with crashing the deadline.

The Case of the Background Material and the Secretary

Hitting deadlines is an important part of professional conduct. I once witnessed a deadline that was missed by three minutes and it rendered useless three weeks of work.

Here is how it happened. A staff analyst was assigned to prepare background reference materials concerning evaluations of state-federal relations for the secretary of a federal cabinet department that dealt extensively with state and local governments. The secretary needed the material as a backup for questions she might encounter in meetings with members of Congress. It was sufficiently important for the chief of staff and the secretary to meet with the analyst and her manager to indicate the kinds of background information the secretary wished to have.

The analyst was so diligent in preparing and rewriting the material that she was still revising the package as the noon deadline approached. Despite warnings about the importance of hitting the deadline, the analyst continued improving the package until it was just so. She delivered the material to the secretary's office about two to three minutes after the deadline. The secretary had left promptly at noon to go to Capitol Hill for the meetings. By missing the deadline by no more than three minutes, the analyst might as well not have worked on the evaluation summaries at all. And the secretary had the impression that the material was not delivered because it arrived after she left her office. The consequences of missing the deadline were useless effort and a damaged reputation with the secretary on the part of the evaluation shop.

How to Proceed

All members of the program evaluation team should understand from the start the importance of staying on schedule and budget. Setting expectations high can prompt folks to act so that problems are avoided. Similarly, team members need to know they have an obligation when budgets or time lines slip to both act quickly to correct the situation and identify the problem to those with oversight responsibility.

What to Watch Out For

No one likes to be the bearer of bad news. If punishment, not problem correction, is the principal response to a shortfall, people will be encouraged to hide mistakes. You must be persistent in communicating that it is much better to share bad news earlier than later. And you must watch closely for people being afraid to bring bad news forward when something slips.

When All Else Fails

All those involved in the evaluation must know what the product is that they are being asked to produce or contribute to, when the product is expected to be delivered, and why it is important to meet the deadline. If people believe the deadline is arbitrary, they are much less likely to commit to it than if they understand why the due date is set at what it is.

BOX 5-3   **Meet the Deadline**

How to Proceed: Ensure that everyone knows the due dates and the resource constraints.

What to Watch Out For: Beware of staff hiding bad news that impacts deadlines or budgets.

When All Else Fails: Accept the time and budget constraints.

GETTING PEOPLE WITH THE RIGHT SKILLS AND TEMPERAMENT

Both analytic capabilities and interpersonal skills are critical to a successful evaluation. When you select your team, pick people who bring the right balance of both. If you do not, you run the risk of having a team of knowledgeable analysts who are unable to work together sufficiently well to get the project done. Or, if you allow interpersonal skills to dominate the staff selection process, you may end up with team members who can work well together but do not have the foggiest notion about the analytic enterprise they are expected to carry out. You need a team balanced in both technical skills and interpersonal skills.

Often analytic skills become the dominant quality used to assign or recruit people to an evaluation. This is both reasonable and dangerous. It is reasonable because the specialized skills of interview protocol design, data collection, and data analysis can be tough to find. Evaluators are knowledge workers, and knowledge workers place a premium on conceptual skills. It is reasonable, even responsible, for someone staffing a program evaluation to give primary attention to placing people with the relevant conceptual skills on the team. This is dangerous, however, because many folks stop there and do not consider the interpersonal skills of those being recruited. The assumption is that while it can be difficult to find people with the necessary conceptual skills, the interpersonal skills are not so hard to find. So if evaluators are picked just based on their technical, conceptual skills, the evaluation will be staffed adequately.

The sad truth is that some bright people have extraordinary conceptual skills but do not work well with others. The kind of talent necessary

to succeed with higher-order evaluation skills lends itself to solo operators. Developing team work and collaboration skills is not one of those
higher-order conceptual skills, so they are often vestigial in highly skilled
evaluators. This can be a killer when staffing a program evaluation. A
major danger when executing a program evaluation can be staffing it with
a unidimensional view to the capabilities needed for the team members
to succeed. A savvy team leader does best to balance technical evaluation
skills with interpersonal skills. Achievement in controlling program evaluations depends upon the combination of both. Success derives from
knowing what to do and knowing how to do it in ways that draw on
everyone's contribution. Knowledge and temperament both matter. This
does not mean that temperament should predominate, but if you do not
explicitly consider the temperament of staff members when you are
assembling the team, you are courting danger.

The Case of the Collapse of the Permitting Evaluation

At one time the State of Fremont's Office of Surface Mining (OSM)
issued a considerable number of permits for strip mining of coal. These
permits were extraordinarily important to the coal mine operators, the
miners themselves, and the environmentalists interested in the projects.
Getting permits issued in a reasonable time with adequate input for
stakeholders and based on sound engineering analyses was a major programmatic and political objective of OSM. The OSM director asked for
a program evaluation because stakeholders were generally dissatisfied
with the time it took for the permits to be issued. The analysis office
assembled a team of experts in permitting processes, engineering, and
management. Cherie Wood was placed in charge of the project. She had
a reputation as a brilliant analyst. However, she had previously experienced personality clashes with others in her office. Wood's boss, Charlie
Burton, was aware of this but decided to give her the project anyway
because he was under considerable pressure to get the evaluation done.
He discussed all facets of the project with Wood, and she assured him
that she knew the methodology to use and would have no trouble getting
the project done on time.

Burton chose to ignore the previous personality problems Wood had
experienced. And he paid dearly for it. About three weeks into the project,

over half the project staff met with Burton without Wood's knowledge to complain about her dismissive and autocratic style. Wood was angering the people she was dependent upon for success to such an extent that everyone who met with Burton asked to be reassigned. Of particular concern to Burton was that Wood could not make up her mind about the data frame, and she blamed others for the delay. This had placed the project over a week late already and likely would delay it further. The successful conduct of the evaluation of the permits program was in peril, and much of it derived from the limited interpersonal skills of the project manager.

This program evaluation blew up because Burton believed that he needed to consider only technical skills when staffing it. Often in an evaluation project there is enough technical talent to assure that the design of the evaluation will be satisfactory. Interpersonal skills in such cases become the critical element.

How to Proceed

It is easy to describe what must be done and equally difficult to do it. You must satisfy yourself that the team members have both the analytic skills and the interpersonal skills to work effectively with each other. This means you must take into account not only an individual's skills but also how those skills will likely interact with others on the team. How to do that is the challenge. But the key thing to remember is that you must consider both. Never simply staff an evaluation based on the presence or absence of technical skills. Always consider temperament along with technical skills.

What to Watch Out For

Do not assume everyone has adequate interpersonal skills. Bright people think that if conceptual skills are difficult to acquire, once they find someone with such conceptual skills the job is done. Not true. Do not be lulled into believing that the only thing that matters is facility with research design, data collection, econometrics, or similar technical items. They matter, but they are not all that matters. Be sure that you think about interpersonal skills as well as technical skills when you are staffing an evaluation.

There is another side of the technical-interpersonal skills situation. Just because you feel a particularly strong personal affinity with some-

BOX 5-4	Getting People with the Right Skills and Temperament

How to Proceed: Consider both technical skills and personal temperament when staffing an evaluation.

What to Watch Out For: Do not assume that because someone has technical skills that he or she necessarily has interpersonal skills.

When All Else Fails: Prefer strong interpersonal skills and adequate technical skills over superb technical skills and so-so interpersonal skills.

---

one, do not allow that to dominate your staffing choices. People prefer to have folks around who are like themselves. Just because someone has interpersonal characteristics that appeal to you does not mean he or she is right for the job. Ask yourself explicitly if an attractive person is a candidate for a position because of his or her technical skills, interpersonal skills, or both. Pick those with both.

When All Else Fails

Sometimes you have to choose people who are unbalanced on one side or the other. In fact, you often have to do that. All other things being equal, select individuals with strong interpersonal, team collaboration skills paired with adequate analytic skills over those with extraordinary analytic skills who do not work well with others.

EXPECT SOMETHING TO GO WRONG

All complex undertakings encounter unexpected circumstances. Conducting a program evaluation is no exception. The combination of complicated public program requirements, energetic and independent analysts, active stakeholders, and rigorous analytic techniques is a prescription for the unforeseen to occur. Prudent evaluators recognize this and plan accordingly.

I cannot tell you what will go wrong in a program evaluation, but I am fairly certain that something will. If you do not build some flexibility into your plans for conducting the evaluation, you probably will find yourself in a crisis mode sometime in the evaluation—and that crisis typically occurs when you can least afford it. Murphy's Law says that anything that can go wrong will go wrong.[1] A corollary says that anything that goes wrong will do so at the worst possible time. If you think that everything will go as expected, you are heading for trouble. What happens may be something as mundane as a printer malfunctioning just before the report is due. It may be as dramatic as your client being fired for political reasons unconnected to the evaluation. Whatever it is, something will go wrong, and you should anticipate and build some flexibility into your work plan.

There is a good reason that things go wrong. Evaluations deal with complex systems.[2] In such systems there may be simple components. However, these components can interact in unpredictable ways. When human judgment and activities are part of these components, such as in the case of program evaluations, the unexpected becomes the unavoidable. The result is that it is impossible to anticipate every possible glitch that might occur, especially when you are dealing with many people working on complicated subjects. However, you can prepare yourself to a certain extent. In short, do not dedicate all the time and resources to the planned work. Give yourself some extra time or save a few resources to handle the unexpected surprise. If you do not, you are likely to lose control of your evaluation to outside circumstances or events. There is no guarantee that even with preparation you will not get hit with something unplanned. But with some prior anticipation you can have some resiliency that helps deal with the unforeseen circumstances.

There is a special category of things that can go wrong during an evaluation that happens frequently: The client asks you to finish your work earlier than planned. Sometimes the acceleration of the schedule may be so extreme that it overwhelms the prudent time cushion you created. No amount of reasonable prior planning can help. You must resort to other techniques.

You can offset some potential difficulty by doing some things before beginning your evaluation in earnest. First, you should try to learn your client's history and gauge the forces operating on him or her. Do these suggest the potential for schedule bump-up? If so, you should have allowed for even more cushion than you otherwise would. Second, you need to ensure the schedule is clear and that everyone involved understands what will be done by what date.

Should a client then ask you to accelerate the schedule, you should clearly identify what changes in resources or assumptions you need to make it happen. Communicate that to the client with the spirit of "it can be done, but here's what it'll take to make it happen." Many times clients assume there are negligible costs associated with shortening a schedule. When they are shown the implications, often they will change their minds.

After doing these things, the client may accept the changes required to speed up the schedule. If so, you must be careful to spell out clearly what the conditions and assumptions are that everyone is agreeing to for the new deadline. This is no time for ambiguity and smoothing. Be scrupulous about what is changing.

Sometimes you face a situation in which a client asks for a schedule change that is impossible. It requires things that are beyond your control, such as release of census data ahead of the Bureau of Census's schedule. Instead of a head-to-head confrontation, use an adaptation of the previous strategy: Tell the client what impossible thing must take place to achieve what he or she wishes. If possible, express this as something that requires the client to do something that is unreasonable: "If you will call Rep. Blank and get him to pressure the Census Bureau to release the data, we can speed things up." If that does not work, you are going to be stuck with the unpleasant but necessary task of telling the client that he or she cannot have what has been requested. In doing this, you must deliver the message along with your expressions of regret and commitment to a quality program evaluation. You must affirm the most important basics, even while saying no.

The Case of the Study of Inmate Housing Costs

The legislature's evaluation shop in the State of Fremont was asked by a group of senators to examine the costs of local governments' housing inmates for the state. The state prisons and correctional facilities had insufficient room to house the felons convicted of violating state laws. Because many city and county jails had excess capacity, the Bureau of Corrections routinely paid these local governments a capitation fee to house the state inmates. Each jail billed the state a different cost, with the range being a factor of five, even though the entire state had similar labor, land, and food costs. The state senate asked the evaluation group to examine this and explain the bases for such different costs.

As the evaluation team assembled the information, it became obvious that part of the difference had to do with whether the local jail charged the direct, incremental costs of housing the inmates or whether indirect costs were included such as amortization of construction costs or administrative personnel costs. These indirect costs would be incurred regardless of the presence of state inmates. The evaluation team took the position that the full cost of housing the state inmates was the appropriate way to go. Some counties and cities objected because such an approach would show them to be more expensive and jeopardize their future participation in the program. These counties wanted to continue to get the state payments and did not want to show any costs that would place them at a disadvantage for additional inmate housing. The evaluation shop fought back, arguing that full cost was the methodologically appropriate posture to take. The evaluation team was winning the battle, which was being waged in the committee hearing rooms and the newspapers. But suddenly the press reported that some of the localities using indirect costs in their charges were showing salaries for deputies that were being recovered two or three times. This revelation changed the acceptability of the evaluation team's position. The team had not expected such a result to appear, and it especially did not expect it at the last phase of the evaluation. Having some flexibility in this case would have allowed for reconsideration and adaptation by the evaluation shop. The team had not done that, so the entire project was abandoned.

How to Proceed

Do not bank on zero problems to finish a project. Build a little slack into your work plan. Nothing goes as expected, so provide some capacity to adapt and adjust when the unforeseen arises.

What to Watch Out For

While you cannot anticipate at the outset what will go wrong, be confident that something will go wrong. Watch for that unexpected situation to arise out of the complex interaction of politics, policy, economics, and human nature that composes program evaluation.

BOX 5-5	Expect Something to Go Wrong

How to Proceed: Expect something to go off-course during the evaluation and provide the ability to recover from it.

What to Watch Out For: Look for an unexpected event to happen at the worst possible time.

When All Else Fails: Give yourself wiggle room by slightly overestimating the time and money necessary to do the job.

When All Else Fails

Slightly overestimate the time and money you believe it will take to get the evaluation done. This is not dishonest; it simply reflects the likelihood of the unplanned occurring. When something does go wrong, you will have some wiggle room to fix it. Also, make horizon scanning part of every team meeting and discussion. Make it a routine practice to ask if anyone is seeing anything that looks unusual or unexpected. This may not allow you to avoid problems, but it will tip you off to their early appearance and give you more time to solve them. It also pays the extra dividend of routinely searching for valuable insights that might be otherwise overlooked.

USE MORE THAN ONE SET OF EYES

Extensive information and complex circumstances characterize program evaluation. It is easy for someone to overlook or misinterpret information. There is simply so much available during an evaluation that the chance of misinterpreting the information, even if it is correctly collected, is high.

All analysts have a point of view. Try as evaluators might, it is not only possible but also likely that some element of bias will creep into any single individual's assessment of the evaluation's facts. When complex circumstances are involved, as is usually the case in program evaluations, the probability of a single analyst consistently getting the facts right and interpreting them correctly can be unacceptably low.

This situation can be mitigated by ensuring that more than one person observes and interprets critical situations in an evaluation. One person may be biased, but it is much harder for two to be biased in the same direction. It is not impossible that both will be biased, but the likelihood is so much lower, it is an acceptable risk. Using only one person's views of data or the associated interpretation can mean trouble; two people's similar views are much less likely to do so. So always have two people observe and interpret critical facts.

The Case of Evaluating Guidance to the Field Units

One federal government department depended upon its regional offices to provide advice and assistance to state and local governments. Because the regional offices were geographically separate and directed by political appointees, they could be independent. To assure national policy consistency, the department's headquarters issued guidance annually about priorities the regional offices were to emphasize. When a new deputy secretary was appointed, she asked the program evaluation group to assess the guidance process for its effectiveness and efficiency.

Part of the evaluation involved semi-structured interviews of regional office personnel who received the guidance as well as state and local government officials who were stakeholders in the regional offices' actions. The views from important individuals in the field were crucial to the evaluation's validity. Each interview involved two evaluators. The first person conducted the interview, asking the questions and interacting principally with the interview subject. The second person, termed the scribe, recorded the subject's responses. These roles were alternated from one interview to the next. At the end of a day of interviewing, the interviewer reviewed the scribe's work. When interpretations of responses were not consistent, the two discussed the interview to assure they were in alignment. In almost all cases adjustments were necessary and fairly easy to arrive at if the discussion occurred within hours of completing the interview. If the review session was left until the next day, memories became foggier and resolution became more difficult if a disagreement arose.

The evaluation team also used the two-sets-of-eyes approach on the analysis of interviews. Each member would independently outline his or her interpretation of the composite of the interviews. These interpretations were then exchanged and points of agreement became the core of the analysis while points of disagreement were discussed to seek closure.

Using this two-sets-of-eyes approach resulted in a qualitative method that yielded insights generally viewed by all parties as accurate, fair, and worthwhile. Similarly, the conclusions from the interviews were generally supported by both regional office staff and their stakeholders at the state and local level.

How to Proceed

If you are working on a particularly critical part of the evaluation, have more than a single source vouch for its authenticity. This authenticity may be related to data collection or it may be related to interpretation of the data. What you do not want to risk is building a critical feature of the evaluation on the judgment of a single person. It might be OK; or it might not be OK. You will not know, and this lack of confidence can be perilous to your evaluation's conduct.

What to Watch Out For

The big danger comes from someone whose judgment you trust. You will likely be tempted to go with that individual's views without verifying them. Do not be lulled into a false sense of confidence when you are dealing with a usually reliable individual. Even reliable folks make mistakes. Do not put such a heavy burden on one person; have a backup. Use more than one set of eyes.

When All Else Fails

If you are not sure about the accuracy of data collection or soundness of interpretation, go look at it yourself. This is known as the Eisenhower approach, after a management practice of Gen. Dwight D. Eisenhower.[3] When Eisenhower was supreme commander of the Allied forces in Europe, British field marshal Bernard Law Montgomery and U.S. general Omar Bradley disagreed strongly with each other during the early phases of the Normandy campaign. Each would implore Eisenhower to back his interpretation of the issue. Eisenhower flew over to France from his base in England, examined the situation for himself, and reached his own conclusion. When you are backed against the wall trying to judge

BOX 5-6	Use More Than One Set of Eyes

How to Proceed: Build all critical features of the evaluation on the judgment of more than one person.

What to Watch Out For: Do not depend upon only one person whose judgment you trust.

When All Else Fails: Go look at the situation yourself when controversy arises.

---

either the validity of the data or the accuracy of the interpretation, adopt the Eisenhower method: Go look for yourself.

KNOW YOUR CORE VALUES

If you do enough program evaluations, you will encounter a situation that challenges your ethics. These situations can be insidious. They do not jump up and down and wave their hands and say, "Hey, look here. This is a violation of fundamental ethics." What is more likely is that a perfectly normal situation slightly changes over time until the question of right or wrong or having to choose between the lesser of two evils appears. This morphing of the normal into the abnormal creates a special need for you to know what really matters to you so you can make ethical choices. You must know what is important so that you will not allow those values to be breached.

"If you don't know where you're going, any road will get you there." This old proverb admonishes us to know what we're about and what direction we wish to head before we must choose. Not knowing where you are headed can lead to doing things that have little to do with program performance and much to do with advancing expedient, not enduring, objectives.

The Case of Walking Away from an Organizational Evaluation

As a consultant on management to a state social services agency, a close colleague once encountered a situation that validated the importance of knowing core values. Her firm had been engaged to conduct an evaluation of an organization proposal for the state adoption program. The new director asked for an evaluation of the overall performance of the program, and he especially expressed interest in the organizational implications of such an evaluation. As the initial data collection proceeded and the evaluation team my friend was running saw the shape of a problem statement begin to emerge, the director asked for a meeting with the team's management. In the meeting he expressed great pleasure with how the evaluation was proceeding. But he then said something that made my friend's blood run cold. "Of course, this data collection and problem definition stuff is necessary, because I want the best possible support for reorganizing the division along functional lines." The current structure used geographic regions as the central organizing principal.

The director went into some detail about how he was confident that what the team would find would allow him to reorganize the division and purge a number of the old guard. This put the evaluation team members in a bad situation. They were in the middle of the evaluation and the client had just told them what he wanted the conclusion to be. This client made it clear there was no room for any other answer. The team members' objective assessment of the situation was irrelevant in his eyes. My friend told me that they realized that they were retained to provide window dressing on a decision that had already been made. The evaluation team's job, in the client's view, was to provide the justification to do what he had already decided to do. My friend's firm believed it had been hired for its impartiality and objectivity, yet the client said there was no room for the qualities for which the firm had been hired. Worse yet for my friend's firm, this was a large client, with a large contract and substantial potential for follow-on work.

After much soul-searching both within the evaluation team and among the firm's top management, the firm quietly walked away from the evaluation. As the team director, my friend privately told the director that there could be a conflict between what the team might find and what he wanted. To save everyone the embarrassment and conflict that might occur, she suggested that the team complete the current data collection phase and provide a terminal report. Everyone mutually agreed to do so. While there were many favorable aspects to continuing and doing what the client wanted, the core value of independent, objective analysis was in jeopardy and that was a value the firm was not ready to put at risk. An interesting postscript to this is that another firm provided the client with the report upon which he could undertake the reorganization and reassignment of personnel. When this was begun, an enormous controversy erupted both within the agency and in the legislature. The resolution was that the original client resigned, the second consulting firm was dismissed, and another consulting firm was brought in by the new director to advise on how to clean up the mess.

How to Proceed

You need to be explicit and honest with yourself and the members of your team about what matters. It might be billable hours; it might be political acceptability; it might be objective analysis; it might be technical soundness; it might be follow-on work. Whatever it is, make sure you have thought about what core values you will not allow to be breached. Do not assume that everyone agrees or understands what these values are. Verify that they do. Talk openly about what matters and why. Repeat play is important here. A single-shot assertion is unlikely to affect people's understandings. Constant and consistent repetition of those core values will stand you in good stead when the unexpected challenge arises.

What to Watch Out For

Do not be sanctimonious. While you may be able to choose for yourself and your organization, it is unwise to harshly judge another person. Specifics affect cases, so unless you are completely knowledgeable about all the circumstances, do not judge. Just disassociate yourself. The only thing you can control is your own actions. Sanctimoniousness poisons future relations and impedes a clear view of further situations that might arise. Most public issues are extraordinarily complex and difficult to address. It is tough enough to address public issues for yourself much less for another person. Stick to your knitting. Do what you believe is right and refrain from judging others. If you knew what they did and were in their shoes, you might see things differently.

When All Else Fails

Roger Fisher and William Ury advise knowing what your best alternative to a negotiated agreement is in all situations that involve bargaining.[4] Put

BOX 5-7	Know Your Core Values

How to Proceed: Be explicit with yourself and your team about what really matters.

What to Watch Out For: Do not be sanctimonious.

When All Else Fails: Know what you will do if you cannot convince the source of an ethical dilemma to change.

---

another way, know what you will do if you cannot persuade the problem party to change. If you have thought about what you would do if the wheels come off, you will be in a better position when they start to wobble as you roll along.

EXERCISES AND DISCUSSION QUESTIONS

1. List the most important reasons for developing a formal evaluation project schedule or work plan. What would be the likely consequences of failure to address each reason?

2. Identify an evaluation that has been conducted for your state legislature. How important was the timely completion of the project? What factors influenced the degree of importance of finishing on time?

3. List the range of essential skills—technical, interpersonal, or otherwise—for a team project you have worked on in a course. Which were most crucial for the project's success? Why were they crucial?

4. If you had to choose to staff a project with people of moderate analytic skills and exceptional interpersonal skills or exceptional analytic skills and moderate interpersonal skills, what would be the considerations you would weigh on each side?

5. Is it possible and, if so, is it prudent to state explicitly the values to use in conducting an evaluation project? What do you expect might be some problems associated with a complete statement of values? When would it be wise to leave some values unstated?

6. You obtain a second opinion on critical fact profiles for an evaluation. The person's view contradicts yours. What should you do next?

7. Under what conditions would it be smart not to schedule in a time cushion for completing an evaluation project?

8. For the case of the collapse of the permitting evaluation, assume that Charlie Burton has come to you in confidence. He poses two questions and asks your advice. You are a colleague of Cherie Wood's and Burton is your boss. He first asks what he should do with the evaluation. Then he asks what he could have done to avoid the problem in the first place. What advice do you give Burton?

9. In the case of walking away from an evaluation, would you have done the same? What are the reasons for your choice? What would change your mind about the decision?

COMMUNICATE WITH CLARITY

Program evaluation searches for ways to improve public programs. But if it stops there, no improvement will occur. People must be convinced of the need to make changes, and they must appreciate the opportunities uncovered in the evaluation. And they must be prompted to implement the evaluation's proposals. To do that the evaluators must accurately and convincingly convey what they have learned so that actions leading to improvement can be adopted. The understanding engendered by the evaluation and the capacity to implement held by the stakeholders are connected by communication.

A well-analyzed evaluation has only part of what is necessary to be successful. It must be communicated so that it is understood and adopted by clients and stakeholders. To have a chance to improve public programs, an evaluation needs a sound technical analysis and a clearly communicated message.

BOX 6-1	The Communication Practices

Lead with Communicating Ideas Not Details
Write and Speak in Short Words with Short Sentences
Preview, Provide, and Review the Message
Visuals That Support, Not Supplant, the Briefing

LEAD WITH COMMUNICATING IDEAS NOT DETAILS

Effective oral or written communications must be built upon concepts, founded upon ideas, before extensive data are presented. These concepts must be supported by facts, but the emphasis is on communicating the key ideas. Facts are useful to the extent that they provide support for the ideas you are advancing. This does not mean facts are unimportant. They are extraordinarily important in developing a sound analytic foundation and in persuading clients and others that the work has a legitimate basis. But, to persuade clients to improve public programs, they must first agree with the ideas for improvement. Evaluations ultimately are about the efficacy of ideas for improvement. Staying focused on the ideas, not on details, keeps attention on the reason for conducting the evaluation.

The Case of the Briefing on Operation and Maintenance of Wastewater Plants

During the 1970s the United States spent more than $6 billion, most through federal grants, constructing wastewater treatment plants to improve water quality. Before the program was undertaken, the nation lacked adequate facilities to treat sewage. Adequate wastewater quality depends upon the operation and maintenance (O&M) of these facilities.

A series of internal Environmental Protection Agency (EPA) studies, newspaper articles, and congressional reports raised the question of assuring adequate O&M for these federally funded plants. At the request of the head of the EPA budget group, an evaluation was undertaken to identify the nature of such O&M problems and possible improvements to programs to protect the large federal investment that had been made.

A national study revealed that both a lack of technical skill and inadequate resources at the local level were leading to O&M problems with many treatment plants. The evaluation team documented this then went on to suggest that private sector contractors could serve to meet the growing need. Specifically, the team proposed that local treatment plants be encouraged to purchase composite correction programs from private vendors.

The director of EPA's budget, who had asked for the study, became a key figure in authorizing the commencement of this program improvement. As a result, the briefing on the issue involved high stakes. Both substantial expenditures and important water-quality improvements were in the balance.

The presentation on the issue proceeded in three steps. The first step was to define the scope of the problem. Considerable data were used to describe the number of plants at risk, the investments that had been made in the plants, and the shortfalls in O&M that were occurring. This phase established the need for action based on extensive data. The second step moved to the conceptual phase explaining the source of the problems. The lack of technical skill and the difficulty that local treatment plant operators encountered locating funding were discussed. Establishing in the client's mind the nature of the problems was the key purpose. The third step proposed a method for addressing the problems, which involved advocating composite correction programs offered by private engineering firms. The client accepted the analysis and endorsed the approach, which became fairly standard for attacking O&M problems at publicly owned treatment plants. In this case details were used to set up the problem, but the problem characterization and solution were driven by concepts. Communication of ideas led to implementation improvements.

How to Proceed

Ensure that the evaluation briefing does not get bogged down in details so that the principal points, the important concepts, are obscured. Put in adequate detail to convince the audience, and keep even more details in reserve should additional questions arise. However, do not drown the principal and associated stakeholders with excessive details. Tell them what they need to know, not everything you know about the subject. Evaluators have a great tendency to want to dazzle the client with their detailed command over material that is only tangentially related to what he or she needs to know to make the necessary decisions. Look at each piece of the presentation and ask yourself from the principal's perspective whether it is important. The client's viewpoint matters in communication, not yours. Usually this means placing the center of gravity of the presentation, oral or written, on concepts and ideas, with the facts in a supporting role.

BOX 6-2	Lead with Communicating Ideas Not Details

How to Proceed: Stress concepts and use details only to support the ideas.

What to Watch Out For: Do not tell everything you know about a subject; tell the audience what it needs to know to achieve your objective.

When All Else Fails: Keep honing your message until you can imagine that your parents understand what you are trying to say.

What to Watch Out For

Do not tell people everything you know about a subject. Tell them what they need to know. You are likely to find many things interesting that a principal will not. In such cases, tend to the principal's needs instead of your own.

When All Else Fails

When you have a complicated issue, ask yourself if you can explain what you are doing to your parents. Better yet, explain the issue to them and gauge their reaction. If you cannot communicate to your parents what you are up to, it is unlikely that you have sharpened the material to a point that a principal or a stakeholder would grok the material. Beware of overly technical presentations. The technicality can mask a lack of clarity in framing the concepts involved that most principals will immediately jump on. If a plain English explanation is not possible, go back and refine the work.

WRITE AND SPEAK IN SHORT WORDS WITH SHORT SENTENCES

Modern decision making in public affairs occurs in settings tailor-made to promote attention deficits. The arena of public affairs is a cacophonous one. Different topics clamor for attention at the same time. Even on the same topic or issue, different players press their views and information that supports those views. And there never is enough time to process information reflectively. As a result, the acquisition, processing, and acting on information becomes a major challenge for any decision maker. If you can make it easier for people to understand your points in such a setting, you stand a better chance of advancing your views. Or put appositely, if you make it tough for people to understand your points, you substantially decrease the chance you will convince them. It is simple human nature. If people have to exert considerable effort to grasp what is being conveyed, they may do one of two bad things. Either they just stop trying to understand the message, or they use up most of their capacity trying to sort out what the message is and then have little left to think about the content. Either way, you lose. Either your ideas are dismissed as too difficult to be worthwhile, or your ideas are assessed using reduced judgment.

Evaluators communicating the results of program evaluations have a doubly tough task. The concepts under study and the methods used to conduct the studies often are nuanced and difficult to absorb. And the people they wish to communicate the results to, their clients, often have claims on their time that get in the way of careful reflection. The result is that, if you are one of these evaluators, you need all the help you can get making your message accessible.

The simplest way to make your complex topics accessible is to convey the topics in short words and short sentences.[1] This does not mean shortening the ideas, just shortening how you convey them. Then your client has an easier time digesting what you are saying, whether it is in writing or orally.

Short words and short sentences are easier to understand and process than more complex ones. People understand complex ideas quicker when they are presented in short sentences using short words. Complex sentences with polysyllabic words require so much concentration that the recipient can use up his or her attention span on the meaning of an expression instead of the implications of the message.

Examples of Characterizing Public Figures

Consider two passages that communicate ideas. The first is an example of the effective use of short words and short sentences. Eugene J. McCarthy, a U.S. senator and candidate for the Democratic presidential nomination, in 1968 characterized Adlai E. Stevenson, the party's standard bearer in 1952 and 1956, as follows:

> *His promise to his party and to the people of the country then
> was that he would talk sense to them. And he did in the clearest
> tones. He did not speak above the people, as his enemies charged,
> but he raised the hard and difficult questions and proposed the
> difficult answers. His voice became the voice of America. He lifted
> the spirit of this land. The country, in his language, was purified
> and given direction.*[2]

Most words were two or three syllables, and most sentences were not
lengthy. The paragraph is seven lines long and contains six sentences.

Barbara Jordan, a member of the U.S. House of Representatives when
it debated articles of impeachment against Richard M. Nixon, in 1974
characterized the president as follows:

> *Beginning shortly after the Watergate break-in and continuing to
> the present time the president has engaged in a series of public
> statements and actions designed to thwart the lawful investigation
> by government prosecutors. Moreover, the president has made
> public announcements and assertions bearing on the Watergate
> case which the evidence will show he knew to be false.*[3]

Most of the words in this paragraph are three and four syllables long.
This paragraph is six lines long, about that of the preceding paragraph;
however, it contains two sentences. The combination of lengthier words
and sentences make the second paragraph, while of considerable importance, more difficult to absorb.

While it is unlikely that a program evaluation you write has the content of either of these paragraphs, clarity of expression through concise
language is a worthy method of conveying complicated concepts.

How to Proceed

Use short words and short sentences to express complex ideas. After writing a paragraph, examine it to see if there are shorter words that might
be substituted. Ask yourself if a series of short sentences would do the
same work as longer, more convoluted sentences that might have found
their way into your writing.

Oral communication has the same needs. If you cannot speak in short, logical sentences using short words, but require verbose oral expressions to convey the heart of an evaluation, then you may not have as firm a grasp on the material as you should. Only those who know what they are seeking to say can express it in short words and sentences.

What to Watch Out For

Be careful about employing highfalutin' expressions that demonstrate your verbal abilities and not using simple expressions that show your conceptual abilities. Professionals, whether physicians, lawyers, engineers or evaluators, who have specialized knowledge often resort to jargon to impress their audience. This seeks to impress, not communicate. It is a death wish to do this as an evaluator. If clients believe you are trying to one-up them, that will sow the seeds for mistrust and rejection of your ideas. Remember, keep your eyes on the purpose: Improve performance. It is not to impress the clients and make them feel diminished.

When All Else Fails

Ensure you can explain the purpose, methods, and findings of your work in two minutes orally or in one written page. To be this concise you must do two things. First, you must know what you are talking about. Second, you must express the concepts in bite-size, understandable terms. If you can do these things, you can be fairly certain that the client will get it and that your ideas will be assessed more on their merit than their manner of expression.

BOX 6-3	Write and Speak in Short Words with Short Sentences

How to Proceed: Prefer two- and three-syllable words and five- and six-word sentences.

What to Watch Out For: Avoid expressions that demonstrate your verbal and cerebral abilities to impress the client.

When All Else Fails: Explain the purpose, methods, findings, and recommendations in two minutes orally or a single typed page.

PREVIEW, PROVIDE, AND REVIEW THE MESSAGES

In communication, whether verbally or in writing, you are more effective if you use a three-step approach: (1) Preview the information for the audience. (2) Provide the information to the audience. (3) Review the information for the audience. Whether you are talking to another individual or speaking to an audience of three hundred, this simple process considerably strengthens the likelihood that your audience will understand and absorb your message. This approach is often known colloquially as "Tell 'em what you're going to tell 'em. Tell 'em. Then tell 'em what you told 'em."

Such an approach has value with program evaluations. Typically these evaluations concern complex topics and issues. People absorb such ideas in stages. You improve your communication success if you recognize this and provide your audience a chance to do what it naturally wants to do. When you preview, provide, and review the message, you have taken advantage of how people engage complex information.

The Case of the Concept Paper on Strategic Direction

Figure 6-1 shows an example of a concept paper that was prepared for a senior EPA executive according to the preview, provide, and review method. The first paragraph establishes the concepts that are developed in the following three sections. The final paragraph, which is presented as a five-star paragraph to separate and signal summarization, reviews the key features of the document. A client who is rushed for time can read the first and last paragraphs in a piece structured in this format and get a fairly clear idea of the concepts that the more detailed intervening paragraphs advance.

How to Proceed

We're often taught to prize economy of expression. It is important to be careful with what we write or say, but we must recognize how people absorb information. Repetition often is the mother of education. We must learn to embrace repetition to reach our clients.

What to Watch Out For

Your audience can be easily overwhelmed with information when you are conveying a program evaluation. The topic often is complex, with

FIGURE 6-1 **A Sample Concept Paper on Strategic Direction**

This was part of a memo requested by a political appointee in the Environmental Protection Agency (EPA). A senior career civil servant advised on strategic considerations shortly after the political appointee took office.

Thought Piece on Organizational Effectiveness

An organization can improve effectiveness in two ways: (1) It can build on the strengths it has. (2) It can modify its deficiencies. Usually, it is easier to succeed with (1) than (2). In either case the emphasis should be on making a difference in those activities that truly matter to the success of the organization.

Organizational effectiveness concerns three interlocking levels:

1. Strategic Effectiveness: The selection of objectives, purposes, and methods around which the entire organization functions: "What business are we in and how will we compete?"

2. Operational Effectiveness: The ability to carry out the day-to-day work of achieving an organization's purposes: "How do we do things effectively?"

3. Individual Effectiveness: How a leader influences operational and strategic effectiveness: "What do I as an individual need to do for the organization to improve?"

In each of these cases there are three questions that need to be posed and answered:

1. *What is success?*

2. *How can we determine if we've achieved success?*

3. *Who is the customer?*

Regardless of the level, clarifying these questions almost always yields insight into improving effectiveness. You may find it helpful to consider organizational effectiveness by asking:

Strategic: How can you influence EPA's long-range choices?

Operational: How can you influence the pollution media programs' choices as well as how [the office] itself conducts its day-to-day business?

Individual: What and how do you wish to achieve during your time at EPA?

Strategic Effectiveness: Great Opportunities But Great Challenges

EPA is floundering strategically today. It has been floundering for about ten years. This is because the command-and-control paradigm, which underlies most of EPA's statutory and organizational assumptions, is increasingly misaligned with the demands of environmental progress. We're relying principally on regulatory answers because past leaders have not articulated and enforced a compelling alternative vision. The accompanying document *Memo to Governor Whitman* explores this in more detail. It was prepared at the request of folks helping the transition team. The paper entitled *Complex Adaptive Systems* provides some of the theoretical take on why such change is necessary.

The agency has made some efforts toward strategic redirection. However, the drivetrain of EPA is regulatory, command-and-control based. You have an opportunity to employ your position as principal steward of EPA's resources to channel resources into nontraditional environmental areas and away

(figure continues on next page)

FIGURE 6-1   **A Sample Concept Paper on Strategic Direction** (continued)

from the conventional command-and-control areas. You also could exercise your portfolio to influence the intellectual foundations to support such changes. But be careful—there are strong forces both within the agency and among congressional and interest groups that do not wish to see EPA change.

Operational Effectiveness: Programs and OCFO Both Provide Opportunities

There are substantial opportunities to improve the operational conduct of EPA's pollution control media programs. Analytic consideration of foundational assumptions can yield interesting insights. The paper entitled *Air Quality and Sprawl* indicates the potential in challenging conventional wisdom. But programs consistently resist probing examinations of what they're doing and how they're doing it. This is not simply a case of momentum trumping change. The programs have a historic pattern of being over-tasked and under-resourced. It's tough to simultaneously innovate and scramble to produce.

OCFO has analytic capability that could undertake quantitative program analysis. However, I expect the programs will resist. The [Office of Management and Budget] initiative in program performance assessment could give you an opening necessary to expand this work. Of course, were you to do this, your managers should ask: "What gets taken off the table to free up the necessary resources?" This could be an invitation to examine OCFO's internal activities to identify appropriate redirection to support the extra work. Or you could take another tack and use OCFO analytic staff to serve as seeds around which the programs could be invited to also provide staff to undertake the program analytic efforts. Regardless, rigorous analytic work can uncover opportunities for improvement by challenging conventional wisdom.

Personal Effectiveness: Nothing Works without It

It is impossible to influence strategy or conduct effective assessments of operations unless those involved, especially the leaders, are individually effective. This requires thoughtful and explicit choice of areas to influence as well as disciplined and sustained attention to those areas. Peter Drucker in his classic *The Effective Executive* says that without the individual effectiveness traits of focus and follow-through, no executive can achieve success. The accompanying *Public Management Research Highlights* has been an attempt to franchise individual effectiveness by keeping individual [Senior Executive Service officials] abreast of the latest intellectual developments in environmental management. Most executives at EPA, however, respond to more concrete influences, such as the budget or legislation. As [chief financial officer], you have entree to all. It is your choice about how and where you will participate. Effective participation will likely require both financial expertise, which you have from previous CFO service, and some knowledge of the programs and their scientific underpinnings. Proper briefing can get you up to speed on those. In any case, asking fundamental questions about important topics can be extraordinarily effective.

*   *   *   *   *

Organizational effectiveness can be approached at the strategic, operational, or personal level. At any level, it is important to ask: "What is success?" "If we're successful, how will we know?" "Who is the customer?" As the CFO, you have opportunities to influence EPA in each area by asking these questions. While you can play in any of these areas, you likely will need to choose which areas to emphasize and how you will exert your influence.

| BOX 6-4 | **Preview, Provide, and Review the Messages** |

How to Proceed: Give your audience a chance to absorb your message. The preview, provide, and review method emphasizes ideas and puts details in a supporting role.

What to Watch Out For: Avoid putting so much detail in the message that the key features get lost.

When All Else Fails: Ask yourself if you have included each of the three key steps.

---

considerable actors, effects, and relationships. The data are often extensive, and the methods of analysis can be abstract. Unless you are careful you can spend all your time on detailed explanations and fail to put the details in context so the client can absorb the material. When you do this, you are trusting to the client's random in-the-moment analysis of your information to enable him or her to reach the point you want reached. Do not leave things to chance; utilize the preview, provide, and review method, by telling 'em what you're going to tell 'em. Then telling 'em. Conclude by telling 'em what you told 'em.

When All Else Fails

Ask yourself if you have included all three steps. You need the preview to help the client establish the framework; the delivery to provide the substantive content; and the review to anchor the presentation.

VISUALS THAT SUPPORT, NOT SUPPLANT, THE BRIEFING

Computer-supported chart making such as PowerPoint and similar software is easily available on almost any computer today. Visuals can be made that have impressive graphics, color schemes, animation, sound effects, and other features. But there is a big danger in using such software's extensive capabilities: You can produce visuals that interfere with instead of support the communication of your message. You need to strive for the message, not the method, as the predominant feature of any computer-aided presentation.

When you are communicating the features of an evaluation, your first obligation is to make it easy for your audience to get the content of the message. Use the minimal features necessary to achieve your purpose and avoid using graphics that are complicated. In short, use your visuals to support, not supplant, the content of any presentation. The primary way to do this is prepare a presentation that helps your audience come to grips with the content of your talk.

The Case of Averting a Horror Show at the Housing Commission Meeting

The housing commission for Buchanan was charged with developing and overseeing implementation of a comprehensive plan for the city's public housing program. The members of the commission were politically well connected to the city council, having all been appointed formally by the council. With more than $10 million in bond funds available to supplement federal funds, the commission was an important player in development of the city.

The planning department, which served as staff to the commission, was asked to develop a proposal for prioritizing housing bond projects. The planning department staff worked for two months on the project and prepared a PowerPoint presentation to explain its recommendations. The primary staff person for the project was enthusiastic about using the latest computer technology. As a result she had prepared a presentation that employed considerable customization features. Sound effects and dissolving headings accompanied each slide. In addition, a considerable number of maps displayed recommended site acquisitions, adjacent land uses, and zoning along with tables of costs, acreages, population intended to be served, and similar information. The planning department staff had prepared a presentation that was comprehensive, thoughtful, and conveyed the decisions the commission needed to make to move the program forward.

When it came time for the briefing, the staffer inserted the compact disk into the computer in the hearing room and booted up the presentation. As she began to explain the first slide, the sound effects kicked in and disrupted her introduction. When she went to the next slide, not only did the sound effects again disrupt her speaking, but she also was using dissolving headings that took much longer to appear than her script allowed.

At that point a commissioner asked, "Mr. Chairman, what exactly are we trying to do here?" As a result, the staffer became flustered and the commission members began to look at each other and get restless in their seats. As the presentation began to spiral out of control, the chair of the commission suggested to the staffer that she mute the sound effects and go straight to the maps and tables. The chair explained that the purpose of the presentation was to give the commission members information on the planning department staff's recommendations, help them make decisions when there was agreement, and identify a need for further analysis when it was appropriate. The staffer shut off the sound effects, skipped the dissolving headings, and went straight into the content. A robust discussion ensued, with the commission agreeing on some recommendations while asking for further work on others.

After the session the planning director and the chair of the commission were overheard discussing the presentation. "Thanks for your help in there," said the planning director. "No problem," said the commissioner. "Next time, let's stay focused on what we're trying to achieve and not get so tied up in the geegaws."

How to Proceed

First, you must know your purpose for the presentation and provide that information early in the briefing. Often evaluators who are presenting material to clients fail to tell the clients the purpose of the presentation. Is it to communicate information in a status report? Is it to ask clients to make a decision? Is it to seek advice and insight from clients? Whatever the purpose is, do not let clients guess at why you are there. Tell them up front.

Next, ensure that your presentation has a logical order that can easily be followed. Almost always this requires an introduction that explains the purpose of the briefing, provides a roadmap of what you will cover in the briefing, and previews the key content. Then, the presentation should have a body that develops each key point logically and succinctly. This section is where you persuade the client with facts. Lastly, the presentation should have a conclusion that summarizes the findings and relates them to your originally stated purpose. This last section should also indicate the next steps to take after the briefing.

For this framework to succeed, do not put anything more in the briefing than is absolutely necessary. Exotic colors, animation, sounds, designs, and related add-ons for the slides can draw attention away from your content. Ensure your slides convey what you want and nothing more.

To do this, head each slide with a phrase that identifies the content of the slide and use short phrases that summarize content. Do not put entire sentences on the slides; key words are all that is necessary, with your oral delivery filling in the details. You can improve the accessibility of your presentation by using personal words and sentences that are short and expressed in active, not passive, voice. In all cases ensure everything you are doing is grounded in facts or opinions that can be supported by facts. And lastly, practice your presentation, preferably before someone who can give you relevant feedback on how you did. Figure 6-2 contains an oral presentation checklist that summarizes the key features you need to strive for in a briefing.

What to Watch Out For

Just because you have the capability to do gee-whiz things with slides, do not be lured into adding complications that interfere with the message. Ask yourself when you are adding something if it improves the chances of the audience getting the message. If so, keep it; if not, ditch it. Also, do not assume that your client knows what you are hoping to get out of the briefing. Tell the client what the purpose of the briefing is right up front. If you want to improve the chances of a successful presentation, clearly describe what success is at the outset and avoid making the client guess what you want to achieve.

BOX 6-5   **Visuals That Support, Not Supplant, the Briefing**

How to Proceed: Organize and then execute the presentation so that the message, not the method, gets top billing.

What to Watch Out For: Beware of computer-generated bells and whistles that detract from the content of your message.

When All Else Fails: Build a storyboard and look to see if the logic of your slides supports your purpose.

FIGURE 6-2	**Oral Presentation Checklist**	
AREA	**Ideal characteristic**	**As practiced**
Purpose	Establishes purpose early	
	Connects all material to purpose	
Organization	Provides an easy-to-follow structure	
Introduction	Explains purpose	
	Provides roadmap	
	Previews content	
Body	Develops each point clearly and logically	
	Provides persuasive evidence	
Conclusion	Summarizes findings	
	Ties to purpose	
	Identifies next steps	
Slides	Is easy to understand	
	Uses key ideas, phrases, words	
Composition	Uses personal words and sentences	
	Uses short words and sentences	
	Uses active voice	
	Has a factual basis	

When All Else Fails

Print the entire briefing on six-slides-to-the-page view. Examine the flow of the presentation. Does it make sense? Do you have all the necessary parts of the briefing? In short, build a storyboard for your briefing and ask yourself if you are telling a story when you look at the flow from slide to slide.

EXERCISES AND DISCUSSION QUESTIONS

1. Under what conditions would you be more effective presenting extensive details in a briefing on the results of a program evaluation?

2. Why express complex findings in simple words and sentences for a program evaluation? Do complex ideas sometimes require complex communication techniques to be effective?

3. Develop a twenty-minute boardroom briefing with data on a program evaluation performed for a nongovernmental office (NGO) client. Practice delivering it using the preview, provide, and review approach. Now assume that, instead of twenty minutes, you have only five minutes as you walk with the NGO executive director to her car. What would you include and what would you leave out? How does the emphasis change? Why?

4. You are briefing the city council on the results of an evaluation you have conducted. Is it better to have multiple presenters from your team with each covering an area of expertise, or should you have a solo presenter? What factors would influence your decision?

5. In briefing a board, such as the city council or the board of directors of a NGO, should you target your oral briefing to one principal or pitch it to several members? What would influence your decision?

6. In the case of the briefing on the operation and maintenance of wastewater plants, what would you do if you were leading the briefing and the deputy budget director asks you to relate your data analysis to the findings? If you sink into the data too deeply, you likely will not get the main concepts across. But if you do not connect the data and the concepts satisfactorily, the budget director will likely believe your analysis is superficial. You had an inkling this might happen because she has a reputation for asking probing questions. What graphics and other supporting material would you have prepared ahead of time to help you when the client raised this question?

IN THE LONG RUN

Everyone wants to succeed, and program evaluators are no different. The motivation to succeed stems from two sources: the desire for personal success and for professional success. A happy circumstance in program evaluation is that they are often interlocked. Achieving personal success frequently derives from professional success. To advance ourselves, we program evaluators must achieve program improvement, and to improve programs, we must exhibit certain personal characteristics.

I have yet to meet anyone engaged in conducting program evaluations who was not concerned with advancing his or her individual interests. It is a natural human characteristic, and savvy evaluators acknowledge this in themselves as well as in others. Evaluators want to get promoted. They want increased financial gain, and they want recognition. In short, they want the rewards that legitimately are associated with quality work. To take advantage of this motivation, we must acknowledge that this self-interest is constantly present and that there is nothing inherently wrong with it. The challenge is how to align self-interest with other interests that lie at the core of evaluations of public and nonprofit activities. Accomplishment is the characteristic that allows us to make this connection between personal success and professional success.

Professional success springs from work that accomplishes organizational or program improvement. Improving effectiveness and improving efficiency of public programs are rooted in the motive to contribute to the larger social good while advancing our own individual interests. We are both individuals and social creatures, and success in program evaluation can enable long-run rewards at both the individual and professional levels, if we follow some basic principles.

PERSONAL SUCCESS

To achieve personal success, especially when program evaluation is involved, certain behaviors and personal characteristics are helpful. These are practices; they are not simply theories. Anyone can learn them, and they are improved only through doing them. No staggering intellectual capacity is required. In fact, their practice is often uncorrelated with conceptual skill. You will not be guaranteed success if you follow these practices, but the probability that you will achieve personal success will increase if you do. However, if you do not follow these practices, consciously or subconsciously, it will be tough to achieve personal success. The first few practices concern developing self-awareness about yourself that matters in program evaluation. The latter practices involve actions you should take to strengthen your long-term personal success. These practices, while not guarantees, are almost always present in program evaluators who are able to achieve and to sustain personal success while conducting program evaluations.

Know Your Purpose

You need a definition of success to succeed. This requires that you have a purpose in mind when you act. You may wish to become the most accomplished evaluator possible. You may wish to contribute to alleviating poverty or improving the environment. You may wish to get promoted to an executive position. All of these are legitimate, but unless you express to yourself what your purpose, your vision, is for success, you are not likely to achieve it. The old saying "If you don't know where you're going, any old road will get you there" is true. Humans are teleological creatures. They need goals to lead satisfying lives. For program evaluators this means knowing with some clarity what our purpose is.

Knowing your purpose does not mean you will stick unwaveringly to it. It also does not mean that goals will not change over time. Successful people change their goals as circumstances and values change. But while the goals may change, one constant is having goals.

Know Your Strengths

Personal success requires you to build on your strengths. You will need to know what you are good at and seek opportunities to use those strengths. To do that you need to be aware of your strong points. These may be technical knowledge, interpersonal skills, organizational skills, communication skills, or any of the myriad capabilities essential in program evaluation. What is required is that you reflect upon what you do well and look for opportunities to build on those strengths. One indicator of what you are good at is whether you find something rewarding to do. Most people are good at what they like to do and like to do those things they are good at. Know what you are good at and seek to employ those strengths at every opportunity.

Know Your Weaknesses

Avoid situations if at all possible that require you to do things you are not particularly strong at. If you are weak on econometrics, do not get yourself assigned as the sole statistician on a complex evaluation. If you are uncomfortable directing people, you are not likely to want to take charge of a big project. You are much more likely to succeed at something you are good at than something you lack skill in. Nevertheless, do not always stay in your comfort zone, only doing the familiar. You can and should seek to improve your weaknesses. When you do try this, do it in a setting in which the stakes are not unreasonably high. Both to avoid settings in which you are not likely to succeed and to place yourself in growth-inducing settings in which you are likely to grow, you must know what your weaknesses are.

Know What Matters to You

Have a sense of what is acceptable and unacceptable to you. Values are essential when you navigate situations that are unfamiliar. It is helpful to reflect upon your actions as a window into your values. The allocation of an individual's time is a fairly good index of what he or she values most. How someone behaves in a trying situation reveals his or her default values. Ask yourself what your values are by asking what you are doing. If you know what matters to you, you can respond thoughtfully to unfamiliar situations. Also, if your actions reveal values you would like to change, you have a clear picture of what needs to be done differently. In any case know what matters to you.

Lastly, knowing what matters allows you to avoid the problem of creep. Creep occurs when you spend an increasing amount of time on an activity even though other matters have a higher priority. Knowing what matters allows you to intentionally choose a course of action that is ethical and allows you to intentionally choose your time investments among work activities and between work and other personal life activities. All of this begins with knowing what matters to you.

Seek to Grow Every Day

Program evaluation concerns skills that are developing and changing over time. Techniques and approaches that were cutting edge ten years ago are standard practice today. You need to keep up with the developments in your field. It is much easier to do this through a continuous review and updating of your capacities than waiting months or years and trying to catch up all at once. Keep in mind that, if you wait too long, you are unlikely to do any studying at all. The amount of knowledge upgrading that you face may be so daunting that you throw up your hands. Spend a little time each day doing some reading in your field. Journals, new textbooks, trade publications, and similar periodicals can marshal the latest advancements. Also, conferences and symposia are fine places to hear the latest developments. But do not get overwhelmed with what there is to learn. Just as in your university classes, it is impossible to know everything that is going on. The field always expands faster than your ability to keep up. Just remember that the purpose is continuous improvement of your skills. Something beats nothing every time. The real choice most professional program evaluators face is whether to spend some time or no time on self-improvement, not whether to spend some time or all the time necessary to know everything. If you seek to grow every day, even just a little, your dividends in personal success will be substantial.

Treat Everyone with Regard

Program evaluation involves judging things. We judge the effectiveness of programs. We judge the efficiency of programs. We judge the performance of staff and managers. That is the raison d'etre for program evaluation.

Because judging things is such an integral part of what we do, it is easy to slide over into judging the people. It is a human characteristic to assess others. But program evaluators, because of the nature of their work, can take this to a dangerous extreme. It can lead to categorical thinking about individuals. Do not let this happen. People do things for what seems to them to be good reasons. Instead of judging and categorizing people, seek to understand others' motives and actions. This requires treating everyone respectfully, whether a supervisor, coworker, client, or interested stakeholder. First, it is the ethical thing to do to affirm others. Second, it will avoid antagonizing others, which can lead to considerable problems.

Live to Fight Another Day

Program evaluation concerns activities that people care about deeply. If strong feelings did not exist, it is unlikely that someone would seek an evaluation. You can be fairly confident that most program evaluations you will be involved with will elicit disagreement among some parties. This conflict is inevitable and can take the form of an attack upon you or your methods. How you respond to such attacks is crucial. In some cases vigorous opposition is the appropriate behavior on your part. On matters of principle or scientific soundness it is difficult to allow a wrong-headed challenge to go unanswered. Just make sure that in such situations you do not win the battle and lose the war. Pick your battles strategically. Live to fight another day. Yes, it is important to stand up for what is right. It is also important to preserve your ability to contribute. Only you, in an assessment of the immediate situation, can make this choice. But remember that not every program evaluation is one you die for. Some are; some are not. In making your choices, remember that it is tough to contribute if you are out of the game. By all means stand up for what's right, but also ensure that you live to fight another day.

Don't Be a Jerk

Program evaluators work in and make assessments of public and non-government organizations. To be successful in organizational settings, interpersonal skills can advance program evaluation objectives. People who are disagreeable, sanctimonious, aloof, and, in general, jerks cause others to resist their suggestions, however sound. It is a natural response by those being evaluated to mistrust evaluators. When evaluators reinforce this mistrust by being threatening and disagreeable, any chance for progress goes way down. A number of studies of long-term executive success and failure have identified interpersonal skills and judgment as a key feature in personal success. Give yourself a chance to succeed in program evaluation. Do not be a jerk. Jerks don't get ahead in the long run.

PROFESSIONAL SUCCESS

A professional applies unique skills for the benefit of someone else, subject to advancing the public interest. Succeeding as a professional program evaluator requires some unique behaviors and practices. These depend, in part, on what it means to be a successful professional in general and what it means to be a successful professional program evaluator in particular.

Seek Improvement, Not Perfection

Do not fall into the trap of believing that you must find the optimal answer to any evaluation question. It is highly unlikely, given the complexity of evaluations, that you will find the one best solution, even if it exists. The search and analysis time required will be daunting, and if you do find the perfect answer, the conditions may have changed so that it is rendered obsolete.

A much more practical approach is to seek improvement as a yardstick for professional recommendations. While a program evaluation may have a single cycle time, most public programs that are the subject of evaluations have multiple cycle times. As a result, an acceptable improvement will be incorporated and further opportunities will be revealed as the program moves forward. You will need to decide if the improvement is good enough for the purposes that propel the evaluation. You do not have to find a perfect solution, you just have to propose a way to make the program better. Enabling continuous improvement as a result of your evaluations can lead to more actual gains in the public interest than persistently searching for the chimera of a perfect answer to an evaluation question.

Focus on Improving What Is There

It is easy to imagine ideal conditions for program evaluation problems. If only people were more competent; if only programs had more money; if only clients would be more forthcoming; if only stakeholders would look beyond their narrow self-interest. These are all understandable wishes that evaluators often have. Unfortunately, most of the time ideal conditions are not present. Instead of spending time on what is not present, examine the circumstances that manifest themselves and ask yourself what opportunities the actual conditions present. Do not spend much time imagining how things would be if conditions were different. They are what they are. Work with what you have and seek to improve that.

Most program evaluators have a combination of conceptual insight and intellectual skills that enable them to see things as they could be. This is extraordinarily valuable in bringing vision to evaluation. But do not let it get out of hand. Apply this vision to what is there. Do not allow an ability to envision possibilities impede actual improvement of existing circumstances. The best way to change things is to press forward with energetic evolution. This requires moving from what exists to what could be by focusing on improving what is present now.

Respect Your Client

People who ask for program evaluations are interested in advancing the public interest. They would not be working in the public sector or have sought the evaluation had they not had some concern over the public interest. Public officials take on difficult challenges. Most of your clients are managers who got where they are by succeeding. They have some combination of conceptual, communication, and interpersonal skills that they have applied to the public interest. These merit respect.

Program evaluators commonly criticize their clients because they behave in a manner the evaluators do not believe is wise. Instead of resorting to judgmental behavior, a far more useful approach is to ask why clients are behaving the way they are. Most people have good reasons for doing what they do. The reasons may be short-sighted, uninformed, or biased, but for evaluators to be able to contribute to program improvement, they must understand these conditions. An evaluator's job is to assist in program improvement, not judge the client.

Evidence Matters

Have documented, fact-based reasons for reaching the conclusions you do. Assertion without evidence is unconvincing. Most managers and stakeholders in public programs look first to the facts of a situation to inform their judgment. Public issues that are the subject of program evaluations almost always have controversy about them. If they did not, you would not have been asked to conduct an evaluation. In cases in which there is controversy or contention, matters of values and beliefs are in play. Those can be framed only through fact-based analysis. A program evaluator's unique contribution in such settings is to illuminate the facts and deploy evidence. Many people can have values and attitudes concerning public programs. Evaluators must look to facts as the anchor that allows them to operate in the highly charged world of public values and attitudes.

Be Intentional

Program evaluators need to look to the sound conduct of their data collection and analysis as the foundation for their unique contribution to program improvement. Execution is what matters. Your primary intention must be the conduct of a study that informs the client through analysis of data. If your team cannot execute the work, or does so poorly, any insight you might have will be discounted. Besides, a report that arrives after it was needed for a decision often might as well not have been done.

To avoid the sloppy execution problem of program evaluation, your intention must be focused on deliverables and time lines, supported by sound methodology. In short, you must not undercut your insight with sloppy execution. Plan, execute, and control the program evaluation through careful and ongoing project management.

Clarity Communicates

Having insight and the facts that propel this insight is not enough for successful program evaluators. These insights and facts must be communicated. If program improvement is your purpose, you need to mobilize others to act. This requires communicating your insights and how you arrived at them. And communication must be of such a nature that your targets see it in their interests to take action. In successful program evaluations the companion to thoughtful insight is clarity of communication.

ENDNOTES

CHAPTER ONE

1. William James, "What Pragmatism Means," in *Pragmatism*, ed. Louis Menand (New York: Random House, 1907).
2. Peter Drucker, *The Effective Executive* (New York: Harper & Row, 1966).

CHAPTER TWO

1. Peter H. Rossi, Howard E. Freeman, and Mark W. Lipsey, *Evaluation: A Systematic Approach*, 6th ed. (Thousand Oaks, Calif.: Sage, 1999), 93–111.
2. Leonard Merewitz and Stephen H. Sosnick, *The Budget's New Clothes: A Critique of Planning-Programming-Budgeting and Benefit-Cost Analysis* (Chicago: Markham, 1971).
3. Deborah Stone, *Policy Paradox: The Art of Political Decision Making* (New York: Norton, 2002).
4. Henry Weinstein, "1st Suit in State to Attack 'Intelligent Design' Filed," *Los Angeles Times*, January 11, 2006, www.latimes.com.
5. Tim W. Clark, *The Policy Process: A Practical Guide for Natural Resource Professionals* (New Haven, Conn.: Yale University Press, 2002).
6. Martin Meyerson and Edward C. Banfield, *Politics, Planning, and the Public Interest* (Toronto, Canada: Free Press, 1955).
7. Kenneth Arrow, *Social Choice and Individual Values*, 2d ed. (New York: Wiley, 1963).
8. Brian Barry, *Political Argument* (Berkeley, Calif.: University of California Press, 1990).
9. Herbert Simon, "From Substantive to Procedural Rationality," in *Philosophy and Economic Theory*, ed. Frank Hahn and Martin Hollis (New York: Oxford University Press, 1979), 65–86; and Thomas McCarthy, *The Critical Theory of Jurgen Habermas* (Cambridge, Mass.: MIT Press, 1981).
10. Herbert Simon, *Administrative Behavior*, 4th ed. (New York: Free Press, 1997).
11. Thomas Dewey, *Liberalism and Social Action* (New York: G. P. Putnam, 1935).
12. Arnold Love, "Implementation Evaluation," in *Handbook of Practical Program Evaluation*, 2nd ed., ed. Joseph Wholey, Harry P. Hatry, and Kathryn E. Newcomer (San Francisco: Jossey-Bass, 2004), 63–98.
13. Rossi, Freeman, and Lipsey, *Evaluation*.
14. James C. McDavid and Laura R. L. Hawthorn, *Program Evaluation and Performance Measurement: An Introduction to Practice* (Thousand Oaks, Calif.: Sage, 2006).
15. Winston S. Churchill, "Address to Parliament," November 11, 1947, www.enterstageright.com/archive/articles/0105/0105churchilldem.htm.
16. David Braybrooke and Charles E. Lindblom, *A Strategy of Decision* (New York: Free Press, 1963); and Simon, "From Substantive to Procedural Rationality."

17. Simon, "From Substantive to Procedural Rationality"; Robert A. Dahl, *A Preface to Democracy* (Chicago: University of Chicago Press, 1956); and Braybrooke and Lindblom, *A Strategy of Decision.*

18. Simon, "From Substantive to Procedural Rationality."

19. Braybrooke and Lindblom, *A Strategy of Decision.*

20. Rossi, Freeman, and Lipsey, *Evaluation.*

21. Richard D. Bingham and Claire L. Felbinger, *Evaluation in Practice: A Methodological Approach,* 2nd ed. (New York: Chatham, 2002).

22. Jody L. Fitzpatrick, James R. Sanders, and Blaine R. Worthen, *Program Evaluation: Alternative Approaches and Practical Guidelines,* 3rd ed. (Boston: Pearson, 2004).

23. Richard Berk and Peter H. Rossi, *Thinking about Program Evaluation* (Newbury Park, Calif.: Sage, 1990).

24. Earl Babbie, *The Practice of Social Research* (Belmont, Calif.: Wadsworth, 1992); and Martin Bulmer, *The Uses of Social Research: Social Investigation in Public Policy-Making* (London: George Allen and Unwin, 1982).

25. William Trochim, *Research Design for Program Evaluation* (Beverly Hills, Calif.: Sage, 1984).

26. Fitzpatrick, Sanders, and Worthen, *Program Evaluation.*

27. John A. McLaughlin and Gretchen B. Jordan, "Using Logic Models," in *Handbook of Practical Program Evaluation,* 2nd ed., ed. Joseph S. Wholey, Harry P. Hatry, and Kathryn E. Newcomer (San Francisco: Jossey-Bass, 2004), 7–32.

28. Rossi, Freeman, and Lipsey, *Evaluation.*

29. Hubert M. Blalock, *An Introduction to Social Research* (Englewood Cliffs, N.J.: Prentice-Hall, 1970); and William L. Hays, *Statistics* (Ft. Worth, Texas: Harcourt Brace, 1994).

30. Rossi, Freeman, and Lipsey, *Evaluation*; and Love, "Implementation Evaluation."

31. Donald Campbell and Julian Stanley, *Experimental and Quasi-Experimental Designs for Research* (Chicago: Rand McNally, 1966); and Thomas Cook and Donald Campbell, *Quasi-Experimentation: Design and Analysis Issues for Field Settings* (Chicago: Rand McNally, 1979).

32. Charles S. Reichardt and Melvin M. Mark, "Quasi-Experimentation," in *Handbook of Practical Program Evaluation,* 2nd ed., ed. Joseph S. Wholey, Harry P. Hatry, and Kathryn E. Newcomer (San Francisco: Jossey-Bass, 2004), 126–149.

33. Blalock, *An Introduction to Social Research*; and William H. Greene, *Econometric Analysis,* 4th ed. (Upper Saddle River, N.J.: Prentice Hall, 2000).

34. Sharon L. Caudle, "Qualitative Data Analysis," in *Handbook of Practical Program Evaluation,* 2nd ed., ed. Joseph S. Wholey, Harry P. Hatry, and Kathryn E. Newcomer (San Francisco: Jossey-Bass, 2004), 417–438.

35. Anselm Strauss and Juliet Corbin, *Basics of Qualitative Research: Techniques and Procedures for Developing Grounded Theory,* 2nd ed. (Thousand Oaks, Calif.: Sage, 1998); Matthew B. Miles. and A. Michael Huberman, *Qualitative Data Analysis: A Sourcebook of New Methods* (Newbury Park, Calif.: Sage, 1984); and Joseph Maxwell, *Qualitative Research Design* (Thousand Oaks, Calif.: Sage, 1996).

36. Robert K. Yin, *Case Study Research: Design and Methods,* 2nd ed. (Newbury Park, Calif.: Sage, 1994).

37. Joe R. Feagin, Anthony M. Orum, and Gideon Sjoberg, eds., *A Case for the Case Study* (Chapel Hill, N.C.: University of North Carolina Press, 1991).

38. Fitzpatrick, Sanders, and Worthen, *Program Evaluation*; and Melvin M. Mark and R. Lance Shotland, *Multiple Methods in Program Evaluation* (San Francisco: Jossey-Bass, 1987).

39. Caudle, "Qualitative Data Analysis"; and Michael Patton, *How to Use Qualitative Methods in Evaluation* (Newbury Park, Calif.: Sage, 1987).

40. Caudle, "Qualitative Data Analysis."

41. Patton, *How to Use Qualitative Methods in Evaluation.*

42. John Van Maanen, "Introduction," in *Varieties of Qualitative Research,* ed. John Van Maanen, James M. Dabbs Jr., and Robert R. Faulkner (Newbury Park, Calif.: Sage, 1982), 11–30.

43. Caudle, "Qualitative Data Analysis."

44. Caudle, "Qualitative Data Analysis."

45. Yin, *Case Study Research.*

46. Caudle, "Qualitative Data Analysis."

47. Joseph S. Wholey, Harry P. Hatry, and Kathryn E. Newcomer, eds., *Handbook of Practical Program Evaluation* (San Francisco: Jossey-Bass, 1994); and Joseph Wholey, Harry P. Hatry and Kathryn E. Newcomer, eds., *Handbook of Practical Evaluation,* 2d ed. (San Francisco: Jossey-Bass, 2004).

48. Yvonna Lincoln and Egon Guba, *Naturalistic Inquiry* (Newbury Park, Calif.: Sage, 1985); Miles and Huberman, *Qualitative Data Analysis*; and Babbie, *The Practice of Social Research*.

49. George Geis, "Formative Evaluation: Developmental Testing and Expert Review," *Performance and Instruction* (1987), 26; Harvey Averch, "Megaproject Selection: Criteria and Rules for Evaluating Competing R&D Megaprojects," *Science and Public Policy* 20, (1993); and Cynthia Weston, "The Importance of Involving Experts and Learners in Formative Evaluation," *Canadian Journal of Educational Communication* 16 (1987), 45–58.

50. Margery Austin Turner and Wendy Zimmermann, "Role Playing," in *Handbook of Practical Program Evaluation*, 2nd ed., ed. Joseph S. Wholey, Harry P. Hatry, and Kathryn E. Newcomer (San Francisco: Jossey-Bass, 2004), 320–339; and Debra L. Dean, "How to Use Focus Groups," in *Handbook of Practical Program Evaluation* ed. Joseph S. Wholey, Harry P. Hatry, and Kathryn E. Newcomer (San Francisco: Jossey-Bass, 1994), 338–348.

51. Kathryn E. Newcomer and Philip W. Wirtz, "Using Statistics in Evaluation," in *Handbook of Practical Program Evaluation*, 2nd ed., ed. Joseph S. Wholey, Harry P. Hatry, and Kathryn E. Newcomer (San Francisco: Jossey-Bass, 2004), 439–478.

52. Blalock, *An Introduction to Social Research*; Hays, *Statistics*; and Greene, *Econometric Analysis*.

53. Newcomer and Wirtz, "Using Statistics in Evaluation."

54. Rossi, Freeman, and Lipsey, *Evaluation*.

55. Leigh Burstein, Howard Freeman, and Peter H. Rossi, eds., *Collection Evaluation Data* (Newbury Park, Calif.: Sage, 1985).

56. Newcomer and Wirtz, "Using Statistics in Evaluation."

57. Floyd J. Fowler, *Survey Research Methods: Applied Social Research Methods* (Thousand Oaks, Calif.: Sage, 1993); Arlene Fink and Jacqueline Kosecoff, *How to Conduct Surveys: A Step-by-Step Guide* (Newbury, Calif.: Sage, 1985); and Seymour Sudman and Norman M. Bradburn, *Asking Questions: A Practical Guide to Questionnaire Design* (San Francisco: Jossey Bass, 1986).

58. Fitzpatrick, Sanders, and Worthen, *Program Evaluation*.

59. Caudle, "Qualitative Data Analysis."

60. Berk and Rossi, *Thinking about Program Evaluation*.

61. Edward R. Tufte, *The Visual Display of Quantitative Information* (Cheshire, Conn.: Graphics Press, 1983); Edward R. Tufte, *Envisioning Information* (Cheshire, Conn.: Graphics Press, 1990); and Edward R. Tufte, *Visual Explanations* (Cheshire, Conn.: Graphics Press, 1997).

62. Gerald E. Jones, *How to Lie with Charts* (San Jose, Calif: iUniverse, 2000).

63. Blalock, *An Introduction to Social Research*; Hays, *Statistics*; and Greene, *Econometric Analysis*.

64. Darrell Huff, *How to Lie with Statistics* (New York: W.W. Norton, 1982).

65. John L. Phillips Jr., *How to Think about Statistics* (New York: W.H. Freeman, 1996).

66. Wholey, Hatry, and Newcomer, *Handbook of Practical Program Evaluation*; Wholey, Hatry, and Newcomer, *Handbook of Practical Evaluation*, 2d ed.; Rossi, Freeman, and Lipsey, *Evaluation*; Fitzpatrick, Sanders, and Worthen, *Program Evaluation*; and McDavid and Hawthorn, *Program Evaluation and Performance Measurement*.

67. Newcomer and Wirtz, "Using Statistics in Evaluating."

68. James Edwin Kee, "Cost-Effectiveness and Cost-Benefit Analysis," in *Handbook of Practical Program Evaluation*, 2nd ed., ed. Joseph Wholey, Harry P. Hatry, and Kathryn E. Newcomer (San Francisco: Jossey-Bass, 2004), 506–541; Henry M. Levin, *Cost Effectiveness Primer* (Newbury Park, Calif.: Sage, 1983); Dale E. Berger, "Using Regression Analysis," in *Handbook of Practical Program Evaluation*, 2nd ed., ed. Joseph Wholey, Harry P. Hatry, and Kathryn E. Newcomer (San Francisco: Jossey-Bass, 2004), 479–505; and Lawrence B. Mohr, *Impact Analysis for Program Evaluation*, 2nd ed. (Thousand Oaks, Calif.: Sage, 1995).

69. McLaughlin and Jordan, "Using Logic Models"; and Office of Management and Budget, "Program Assessment Rating Tool," www.whitehouse.gov/omb/part/index.html.

CHAPTER FOUR

1. Rudyard Kipling, *The Just-So Stories* (London, England: Random House, 1902).

2. Peter J. Haas and J. Fred Springer, *Applied Policy Research: Concepts and Cases* (New York: Garland, 1998), 161–184.

3. Joseph S. Wholey, Harry P. Hatry, and Kathryn E. Newcomer, eds., *Handbook of Practical Program Evaluation* (San Francisco: Jossey-Bass, 2004).
4. Steven Cohen and Ronald Brand, *Total Quality Management in Government* (San Francisco: Jossey-Bass, 1993).
5. Wholey, Hatry, and Newcomer, *Handbook of Practical Program Evaluation.*
6. Peter Drucker, *The Effective Executive* (New York: Harper & Row, 1966).

CHAPTER FIVE

1. Arthur Bloch, *Murphy's Law: The 26th Anniversary Edition* (New York: Penguin, 2003).
2. Klaus Mainzer, *Thinking in Complexity* (Berlin, Germany: Springer, 1996).
3. Stephen E. Ambrose, *Eisenhower: Soldier, General of the Army, President-Elect, 1890–1952* (New York: Simon and Schuster, 1983).
4. Roger Fisher and William Ury, *Getting to Yes* (New York: Houghton Mifflin, 1981).

CHAPTER SIX

1. Rudolf Flesch, *The Art of Readable Writing* (New York: Harper and Row, 1974).
2. Eugene J. McCarthy, "An Indefensible War," in *Great American Speeches,* ed. Gregory R. Suriano (New York: Gramercy Books, 1993), 244–248.
3. Barbara Jordan, "On the Impeachment of the President," in *Great American Speeches,* ed. Gregory R. Suriano (New York: Gramercy Books, 1993), 281–286.

INDEX

References to boxes, figures, notes, and tables are indicated by b, f, n, and t.